a manual for making, ideas and experiences

a performance script

To Sascha

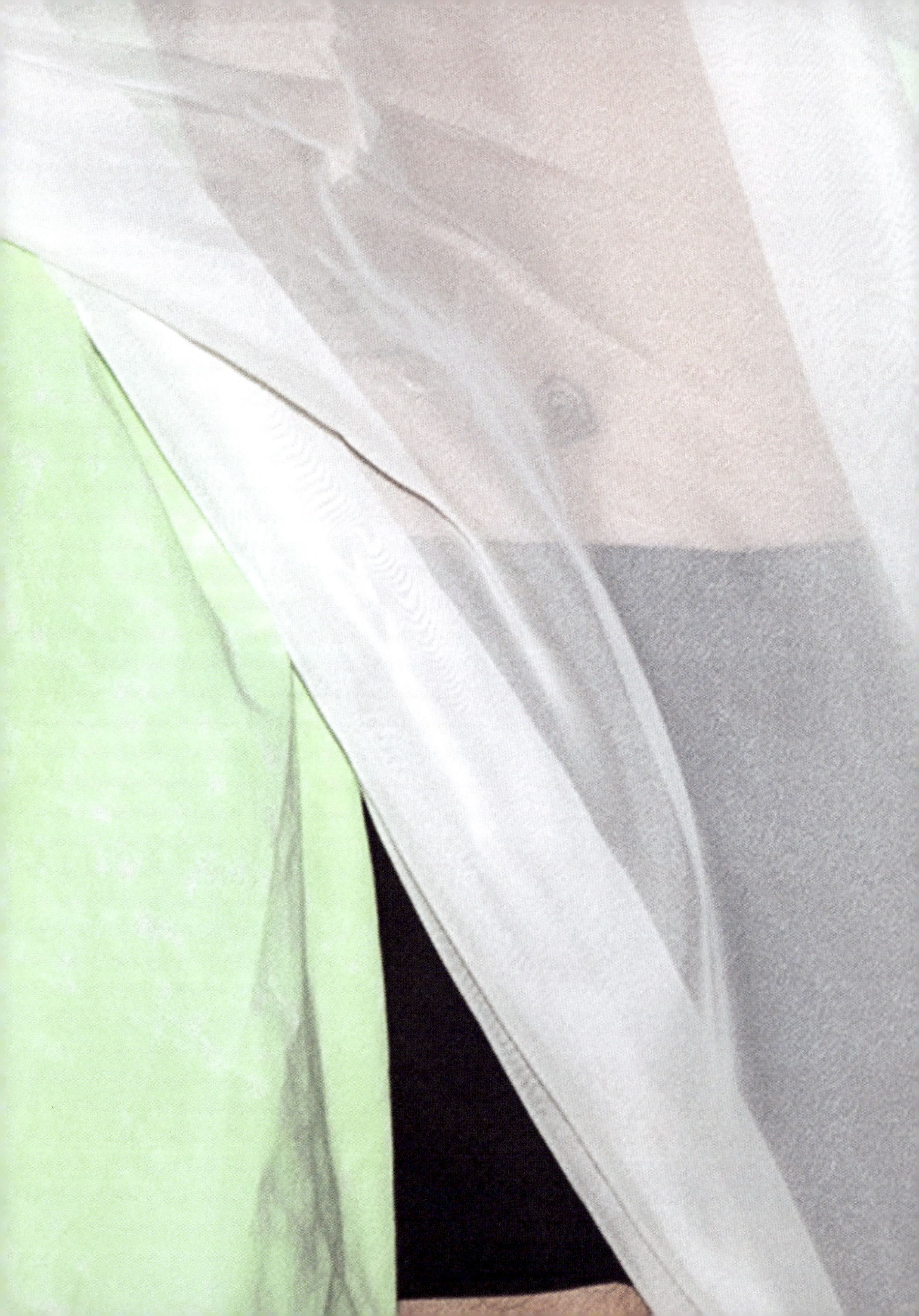

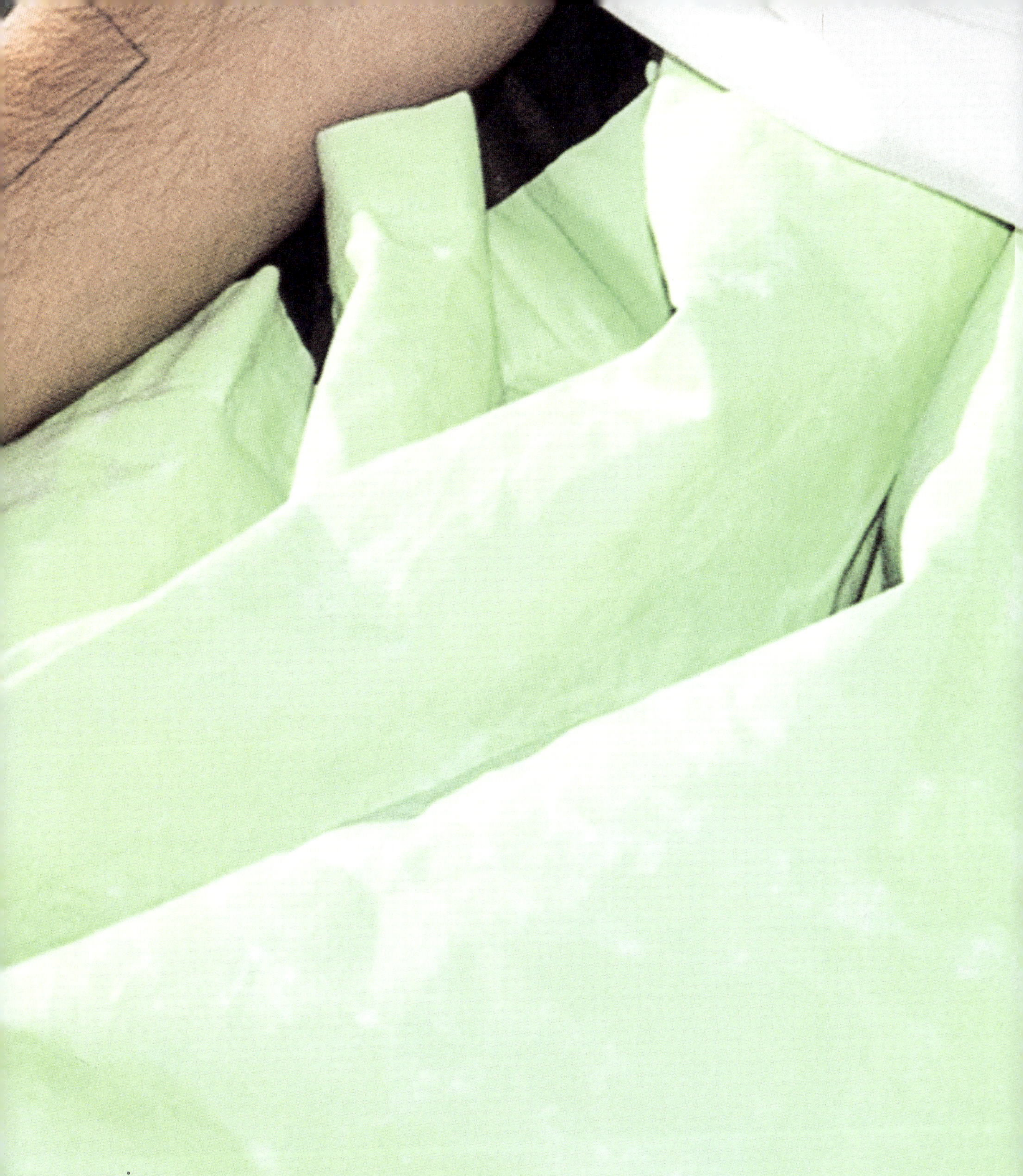

Maxime:

The Agender costume feels pleasant and comforting, requiring a little time to "tame" and shape to our liking, but once we do, there's a sense of pride in being able to parade around in it.

This "What's Going On?" Parade encapsulates the spirit of self-exclusion, offering participants a path to personal fulfilment while reconnecting them with their authentic desires. It encourages critical thinking, breaks the chains of conformity, and empowers individuals to challenge societal norms. Through this collective act of liberation, the parade becomes a powerful catalyst for social change, inviting onlookers to confront their biases and embrace the beauty of human diversity.

Beyond the manual, the book showcases $t^{an}gib_{le}$ examples of this remake and activation, as queer students from the Ringling College of Art and Design in Sarasota brought the project to life. A second activation during the three-day Horst Festival for Music and Art in Vilvoorde further illustrates the project's reach. This experiment culminated in a letter from the participants at Horst to the creators of the costume at Ringling College, continuing the project's collective journey. Several of these letters are included in the conclusion, symbolizing the ongoing construction of community through shared artistic expression.

Let's discover this together!

LDB

Brussels, autumn 2024

Dear reader,

This publication, "Breaking Free: Queer Temporality and Collaborative Art " delves into the transformative concept of self-exclusion, a conscious choice to withdraw from societal norms and expectations. This deliberate distancing, often overshadowed by the dominant culture's obsession with recognition, fosters profound self-awareness and a richer sense of purpose.

By stepping outside mainstream society, self-exclusion opens the door to new opportunities and experiences. It allows individuals to reconnect with their deepest passions and desires, unburdened by the need for external approval. This freedom nurtures curiosity and critical thinking, encouraging the exploration of ideas without the constraints of judgment. In the process, a more independent identity emerges—one free from societal power dynamics—leading to greater autonomy and personal empowerment.

This publication serves as a practical guide to experiencing self-exclusion through the "What's Going On?" Parade. It provides instructions for recreating Hélio Oiticica's iconic artwork "Parangolé Capa 21, Xoxoba" and includes a Performance Specification Form to activate this work in the parade setting.

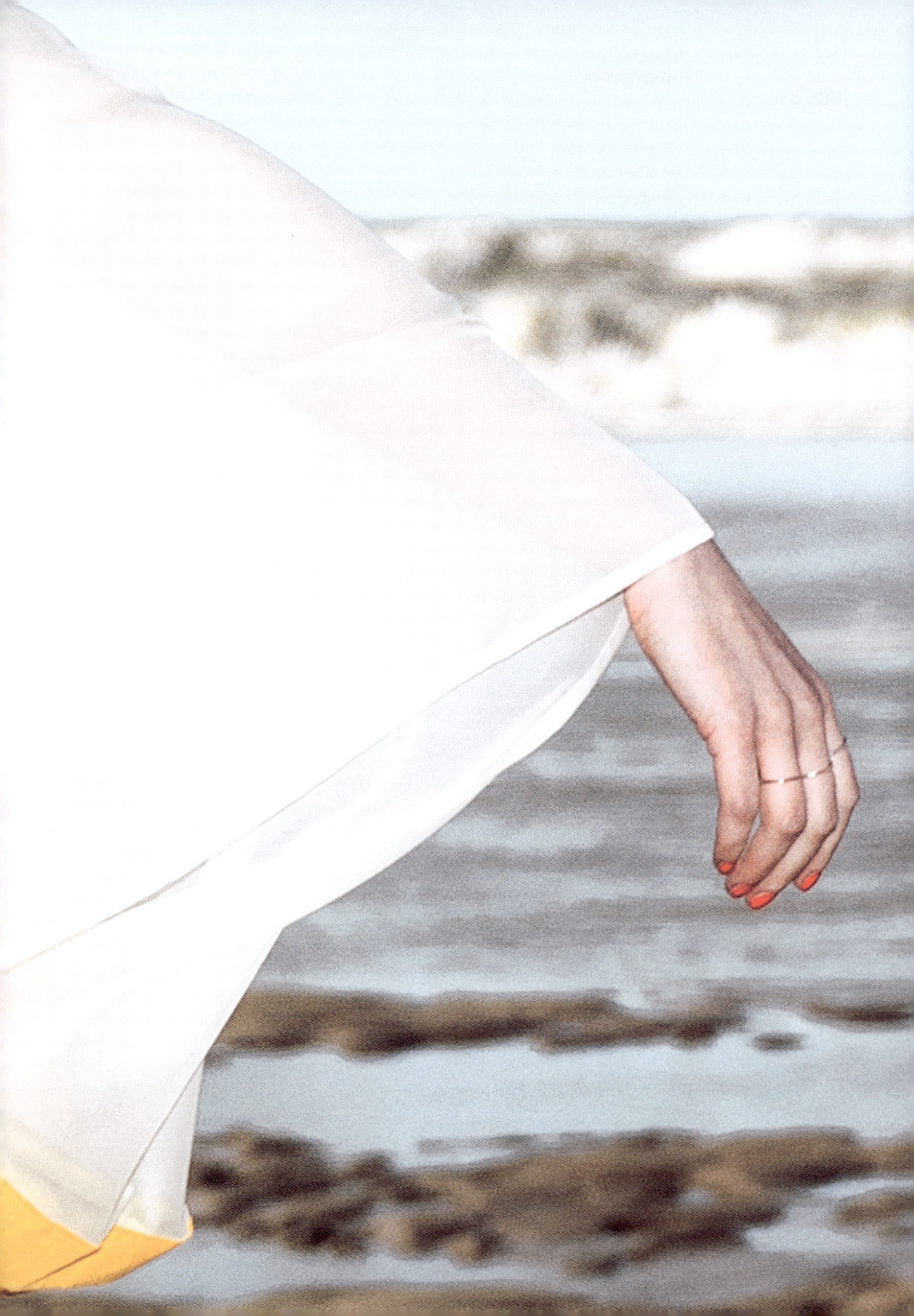

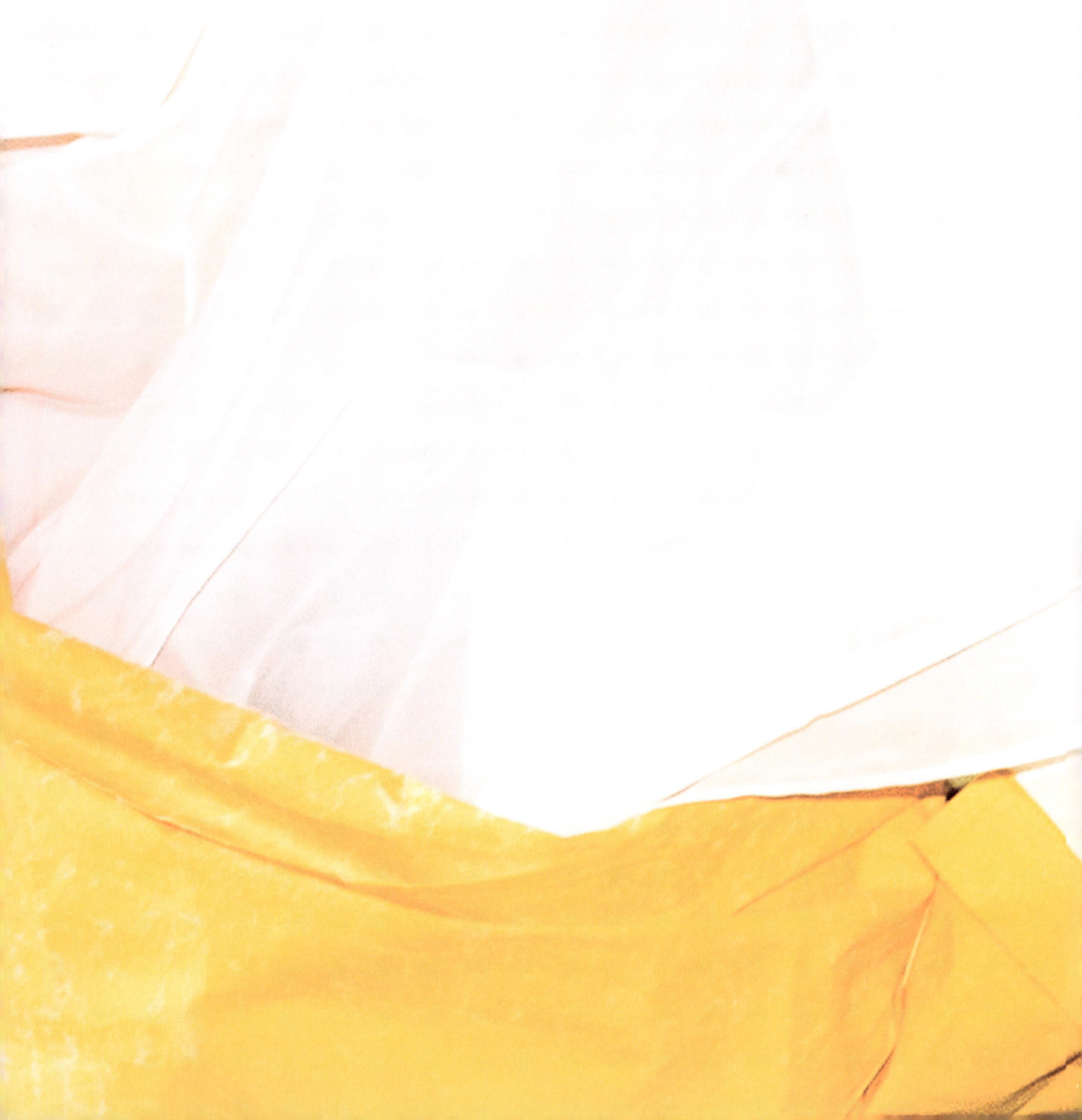

Anne-Sophie:

It was a collective experience of wearing and feeling, where we let go —though with some hesitation—of the individual costumes we each wear and express a queer identity. In their place, we embraced a different fabric, one that was open, uninhibited, and centered on the group. Its sensuality freed us from our everyday selves, drawing us into a new, intimate sense of communion, a shared connection that felt liberating and transformative.

situations, only to reappear when the context allows for our true selves to emerge. This pattern applies to art as well.

While art is often commodified, its essence lies outside the economic demand for production. Art is created out of a need for expression, exploration, or provocation, not for financial gain. This refusal to conform to the logic of productivity can be seen as inherently queer. The challenge for an artwork, much like for a queer person, is to maintain its authenticity when it reappears in a neoliberal art market that tries to commodify it. The context in which it is presented must allow the artwork to retain its original intent, just as queer individuals need spaces that let them be their true selves. A queer, post-productive approach to artistic research can help foster such contexts.

Disappearance has been a constant presence in my life as a queer person since I was seven years old. Going back to my parents' home meant daily acts of self-erasure, concealing parts of myself to survive in a world that didn't accept me.

My expressions of femininity, once inno-cent and joyful, were increasingly suppressed, forcing me into a performance of survival. Growing up meant conforming to the expectations of a neoliberal, heteronormative society, where critical readings of otherness were only tolerated in spaces like comedy, fairy tales, or LGBTQIA+ events. Even in spaces like Carnaval or Pride, these moments of acceptance were fleeting. Outside of them,

Letter to the Artworld, Let's go Queer!

During the past 15 years, my artistic practice has been guided by the deeply personal and emotionally charged concept of The Archive of Disappearance, which emerged from a conversation with art historian Verena Konrad in 2009. This title initially came from the material nature of my work: showing things by erasing them, making certain elements disappear, and arranging these works into an installation similar to an archive. Over time, the entirety of my works began to form this Archive of Disappearance. Today, 15 years later, I understand its significance in a different way—one that is intertwined with my experience as a queer person.

The past four years of exploring concepts and ideas from other artists and theorists have felt like a process of returning home. I've come to understand the pressures, stresses, and creative impulses that have shaped both my life and my art.
The restrictions I placed on myself to fit into society have been both a limitation and a driving force in my creative journey. My strategy of disappearance, rooted in personal experience, now informs how I understand the broader art world, showing how artworks can disappear and reappear in new con-texts.

This constant cycle of disappearance and reappearance echoes the survival strategies queer individuals often adopt to survive in a heteronormative society. We learn to disappear in certain

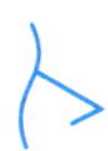

should be asking is: when is art?

Artistic research through a queer lens—particularly by explor-
ing the question "when is art?"—offers a way to experience art
in a fundamentally different way. This approach uses a unique
temporality, much like the queer knowledge of cruising, which
seeks encounters rooted in equality. Cruising represents a break
from linear time, intertwining past, present, and future in a way
that contrasts with the rigid frameworks of traditional academ-
ic research. It is about creating a momentary space where queer
identities and experiences can exist freely, unbound by societal
expectations.

Similarly, queer temporality allows for the reappearance and
reactivation of artworks in ways that traditional methods
cannot. When we ask "when is art?" through a queer lens, we
open a space where art exists in a state of constant becoming—
continuously reshaped by the desires and interactions of those
who engage with it. This kind of dynamic engagement isn't tied
to the original context or the artist's intent but evolves over
time, offering new insights and connections.

This queer approach frees us from the constraints of
traditional art history, which often prioritizes linear
narratives, authorial intent, and historical context. Instead,
queer methodology embraces fluidity, spontaneity, and the
multiplicity of voices that contribute to an artwork's meaning.

queer identities are often forced to disappear once again.
In this sense, my life—and the lives of many other queer
people—can be understood as an archive of disappearance. It
consists of disconnected moments in time when we can be ourselves, surrounded by long stretches of enforced invisibility in
order to function in a society that demands conformity. These
queer moments form a collection of present experiences that do
not follow a linear history but rather exist as moments of re-
appearance. Meanwhile, there is constant pressure for queer
lives to be normalized through heteronormative concepts like
marriage, adoption, or assimilation into mainstream society,
where the "other" must either be normalized or disappear. This
play of appearance and dis- appearance works as a mirror:
for queer persons to appear in heteronormative society, they
must make themselves disappear; and when queer persons can
appear and be themselves, they disappear for heteronormative
society.

This dynamic also exists within the art world. An artwork is
initially created in the safe space of the artist's studio or in its
original context. The first public presentation of the artwork
shapes how it is understood. But once that moment is over, both
the artwork and its original context recede into an archive of
disappearance. When the artwork is exhibited again in a new
time and place, the new context must allow for an authentic
experience of the work as intended by the artist. Otherwise,
the work risks losing its true meaning. The critical question we

It encourages us to celebrate the diversity, spontaneity, and 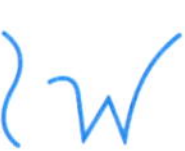
transformative power of art in shaping our identities and
communities.

This queer approach is particularly relevant in the current art
world, where much contemporary art has shifted from being
provocative and challenging to merely illustrative. Many works
today, even those tackling important themes like identity,
politics, and   social justice, often feel diluted—designed
to fit with-   in market trends or to satisfy institutional
expectations. Rather than being spaces for disruption or criti-
cal inquiry, they risk becoming easy reflections of current nar-
ratives, palatable to mainstream audiences. A queer approach
challenges this complacency. It reinvigorates art's role as a force
for questioning, for unsettling norms, and for pushing beyond
the commodification of ideas. By applying queer temporali-
ty and methods, we can resist the pressures of conformity and
reclaim art as a space of true provocation, one that invites fresh
dialogues, unexpected encounters, and deeper engagements with
the world.

Let's go queer,
embracing the radical potential   of art to transform,
to question, and to reimagine   the world around us.

LDB +

Each engagement with art becomes a unique, personal experience where emotions and perspectives play a crucial role. Moreover, this queer art research encourages us to critically examine the power structures and exclusions present within the art world. It challenges norms of representation and visibility, particularly for marginalized communities whose voices are often silenced. By adopting a queer lens, we create a more inclusive and equitable art world.

In 2023, I recreated and activated a copy of Parangolé Capa 21, Xoxoba *by Hélio Oiticica. This experience taught me that art can convey powerful messages while being experiential and interactive. Oiticica, a queer artist, aimed to bring marginalized people of the favelas into public space, drawing from his own understanding of exclusion as a queer individual.*
By reactivating his work today, I've witnessed how his radical, queer temporality—what Jean-Luc Nancy describes as a pure coming of the present continues to challenge and invigorate our understanding of art. This queer return to Oiticica's work brings it out of the archive of disappearance and into a space where its transformative potential can still resonate and disrupt, reflecting how art and queerness continuously reappear and redefine *themselves in our present moment.*

In the art world, this queer temporality allows us to engage with art as a living experience rather than a relic of the past.

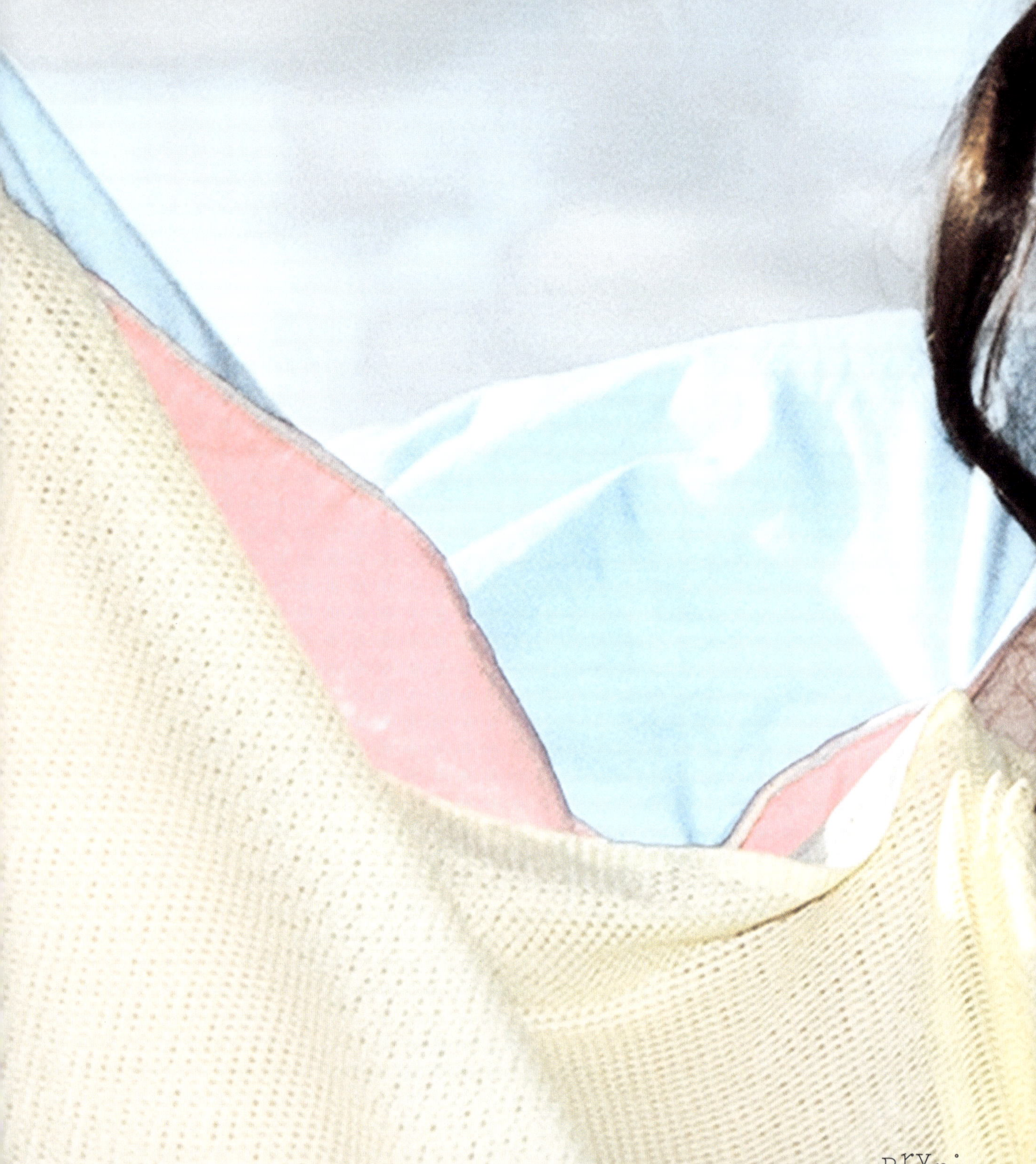

Bryn:

As the fabric of the genderflux costume settles on my shoulders,
I find a sense of balance.
The moment I let go and trust my senses, an enjoyable
feeling comes within reach.

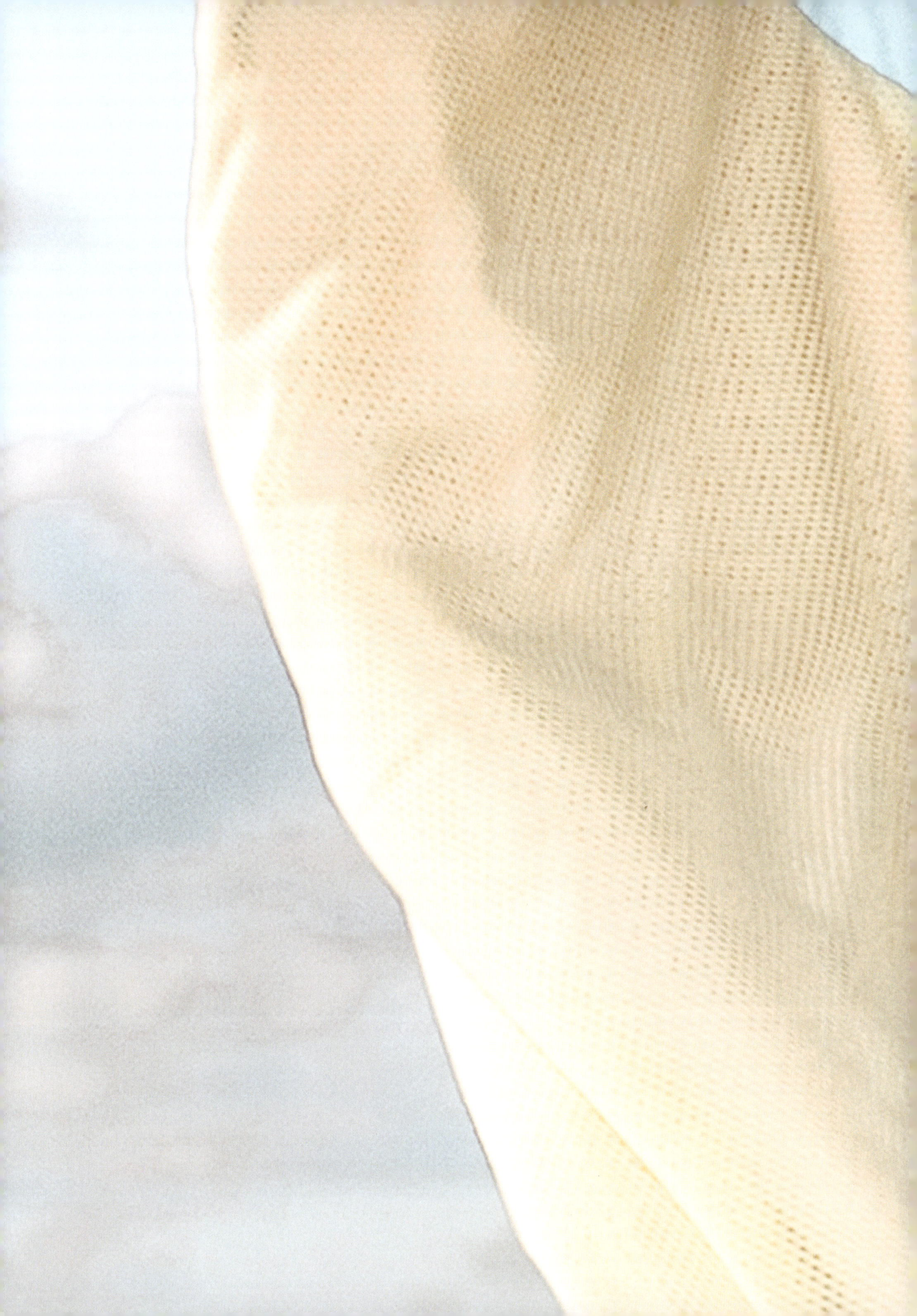

PARANGOLE 3 PATTERN PIECES

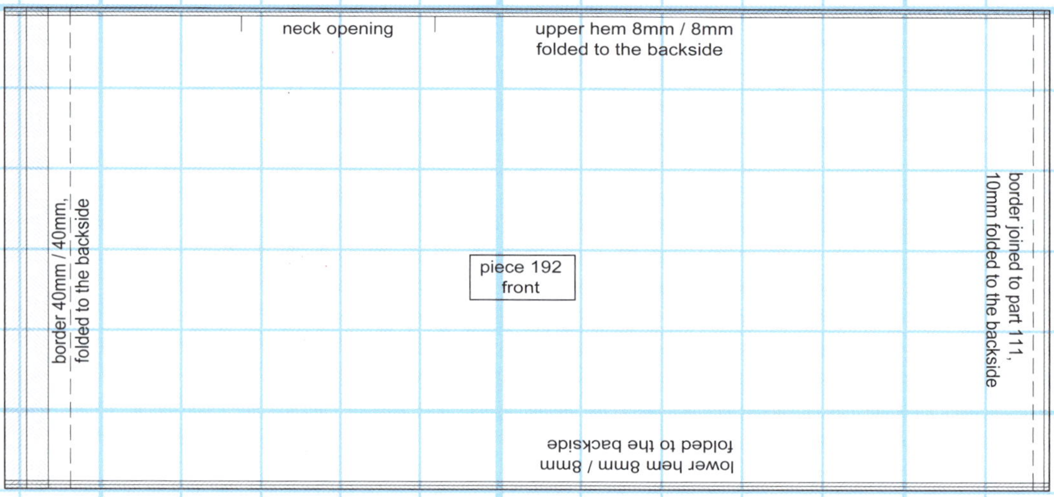

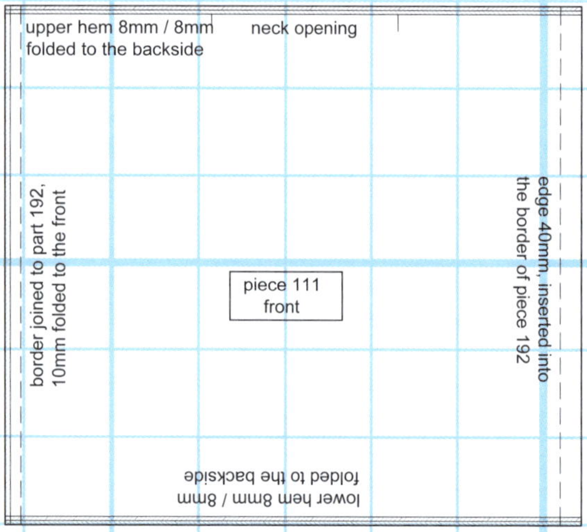

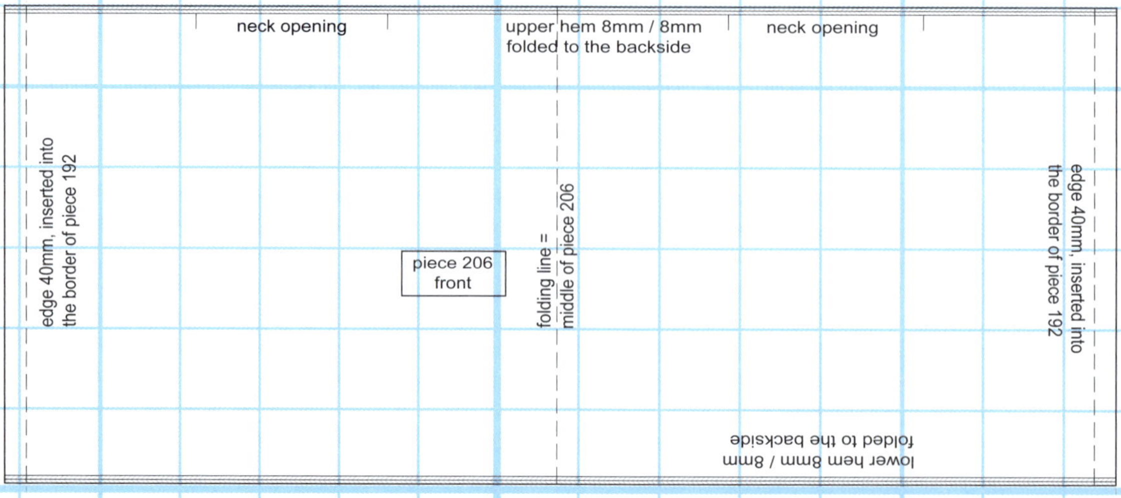

neck opening

upper hem 8mm / 8mm
folded to the backside

border 40mm / 40mm,
folded to the backside

piece 192
front

border joined to part 111,
10mm folded to the backside

lower hem 8mm / 8mm
folded to the backside

upper hem 8mm / 8mm
folded to the backside

neck opening

border joined to part 192,
10mm folded to the front

piece 111
front

edge 40mm, inserted into
the border of piece 192

lower hem 8mm / 8mm
folded to the backside

neck opening

upper hem 8mm / 8mm
folded to the backside

neck opening

edge 40mm, inserted into
the border of piece 192

piece 206
front

folding line =
middle of piece 206

edge 40mm, inserted into
the border of piece 192

lower hem 8mm / 8mm
folded to the backside

a manual for making

1. COMPOSITION OUT OF 3 PIECES OF FABRIC

the Copy of the Original Copy of Capa 21, Xoxoba, of Hélio Oiticica

The COOCCAPA21, Xoxoba is composed out of three pieces of fabric.

On the right page you find the dimensions and pattern drawings for each fabric. These include the elements that are guiding the sewing instructions in chapter 2.

The drawings show the front (good side) of the fabric, seam allowances included (hatched parts). Units: mm/cm

Pattern pieces are named after their width, resulting in: piece 111 / piece 192 / piece 206

When using different colors of fabrics, make sure the correct colors are used for the top and bottom threads in the machine.

Piece 111 and 192 will form one long strip, turned in and around piece 206.

1.3 fabric 206

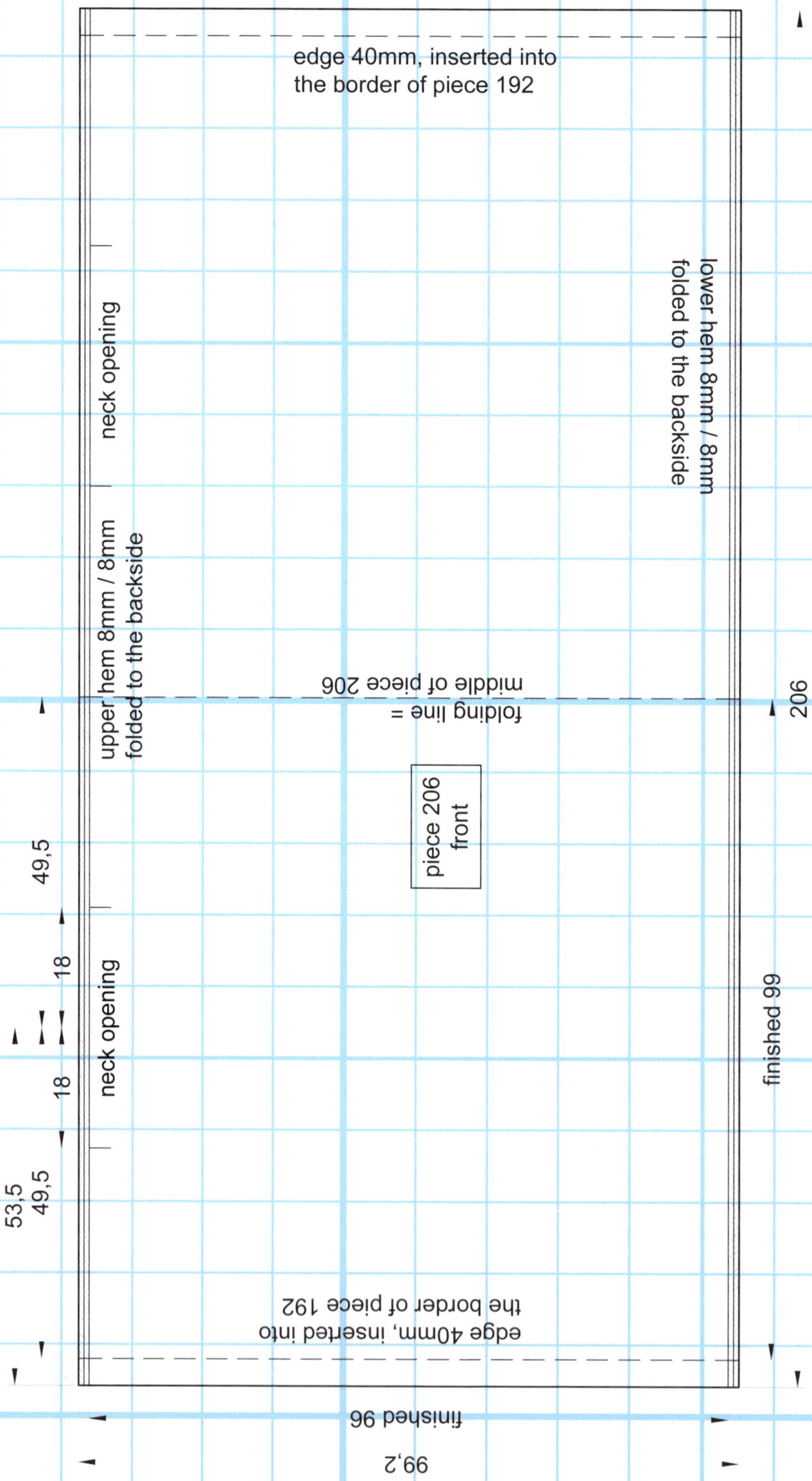

edge 40mm, inserted into
the border of piece 192

neck opening

lower hem 8mm / 8mm
folded to the backside

upper hem 8mm / 8mm
folded to the backside

middle of piece 206
folding line =

piece 206
front

49,5

18

18

49,5

53,5

206

finished 99

neck opening

edge 40mm, inserted into
the border of piece 192

finished 96

99,2

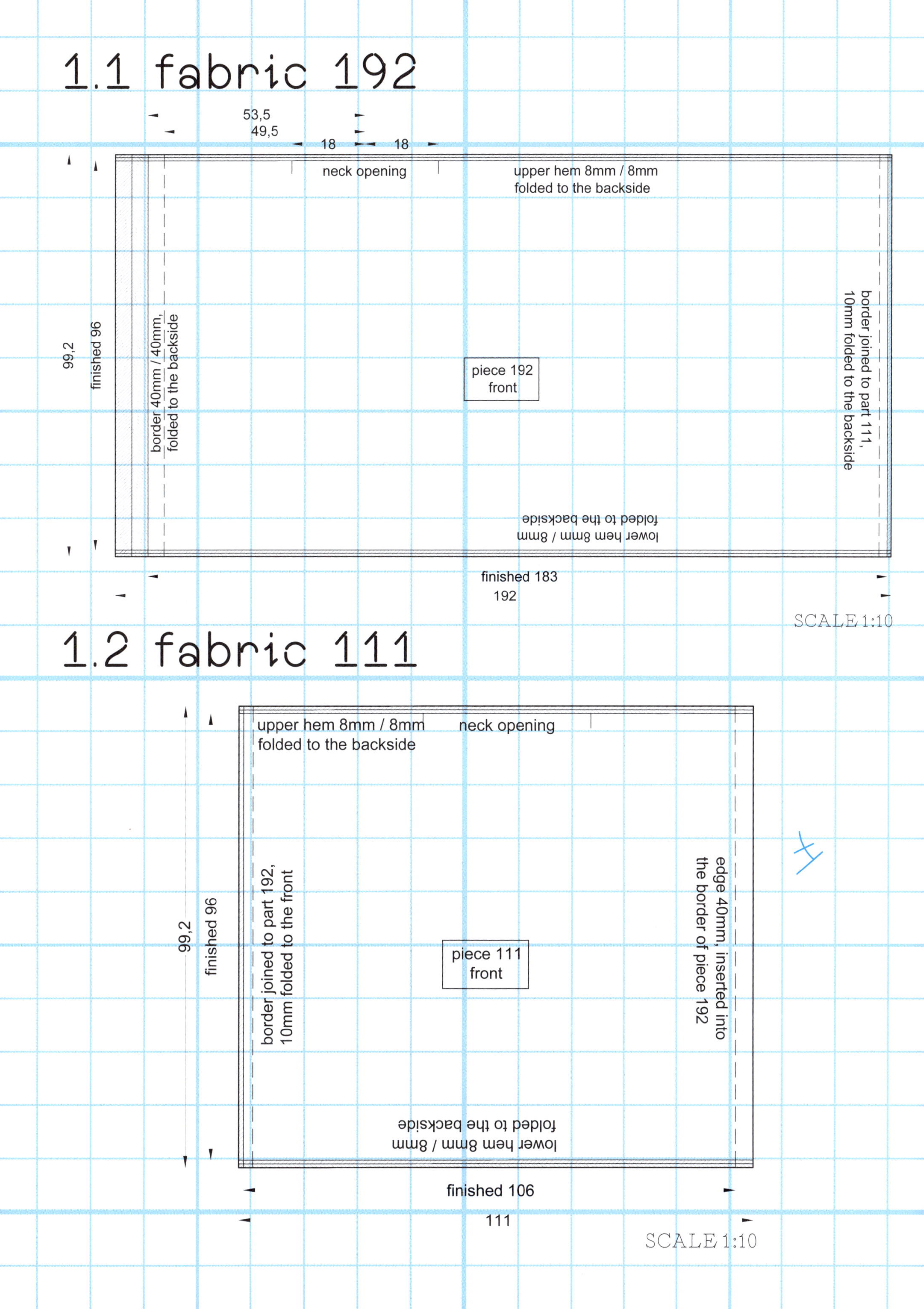

1.1 fabric 192
53,5
49,5
18
18
neck opening
upper hem 8mm / 8mm
folded to the backside
border joined to part 111,
10mm folded to the backside
border 40mm / 40mm,
folded to the backside
99,2
finished 96
piece 192
front
lower hem 8mm / 8mm
folded to the backside
finished 183
192
SCALE 1:10
1.2 fabric 111
upper hem 8mm / 8mm
folded to the backside
neck opening
border joined to part 192,
10mm folded to the front
99,2
finished 96
piece 111
front
edge 40mm, inserted into
the border of piece 192
lower hem 8mm / 8mm
folded to the backside
finished 106
111
SCALE 1:10

(3) Stitch on the edge of the hem. Make sure to
use the correct colors for the top and bottom
threads in the machine.

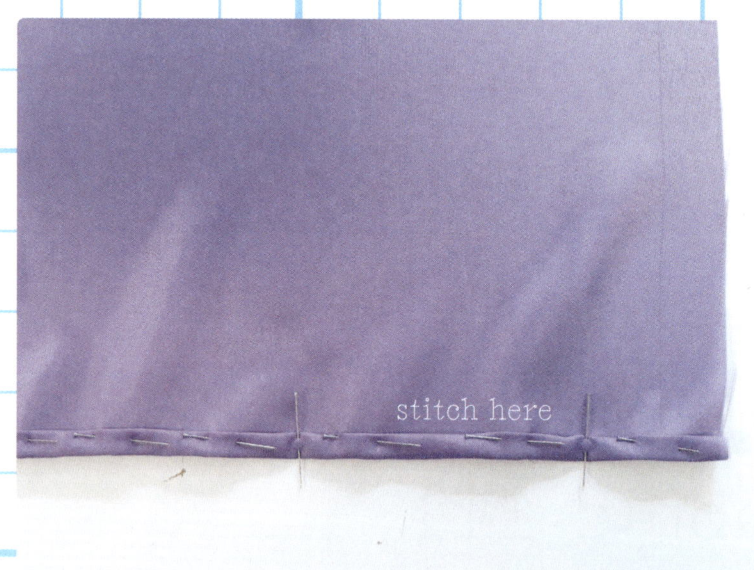

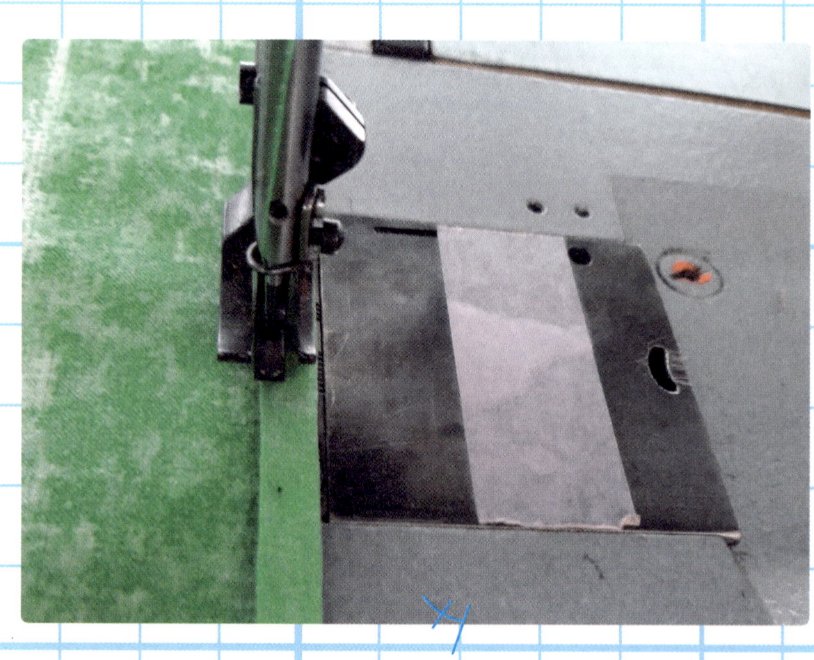

2. SEWING GUIDE IN 7 STEPS

2.1 cutting

(1) Cut all 3 pieces (111, 192 and 206).
The seam allowances are included and drawn on
the pattern.

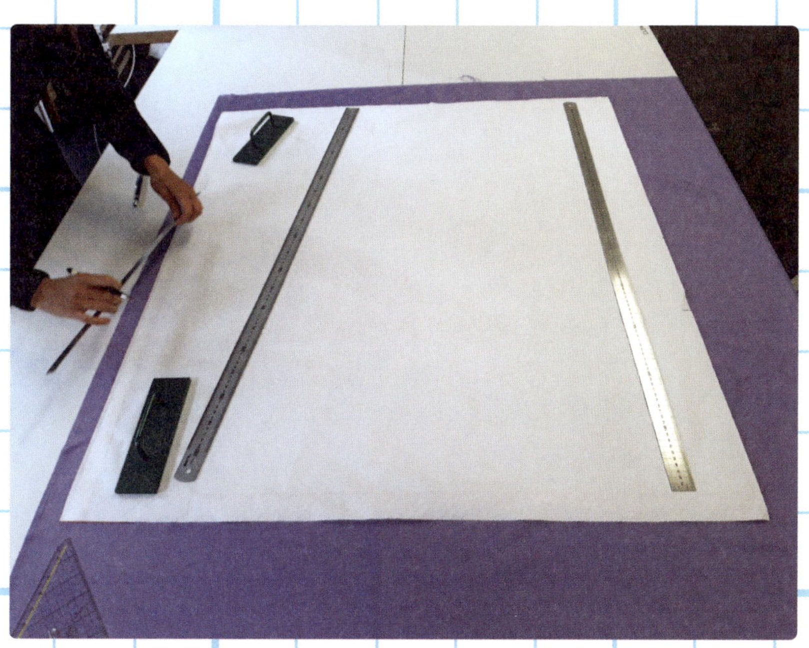

2.2 finishing the hems

(1) (2) Finish both hems, upper and lower, of
each piece (111, 192 and 206) with an 8mm double
folded hem (fold to the back of the fabric). If
necessary, draw guide lines on the back of the
fabric (e.g. at 16mm).

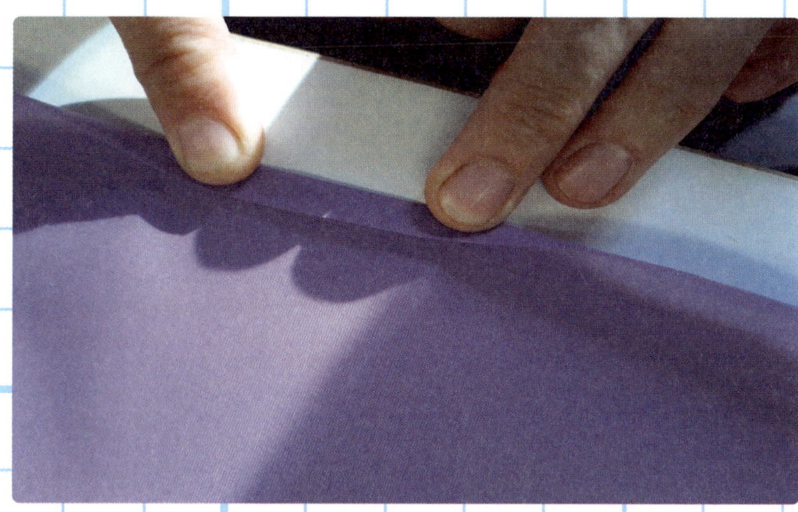

(3) After stitching: turn piece 111 over the stitch,
covering the stitch and both folded edges.

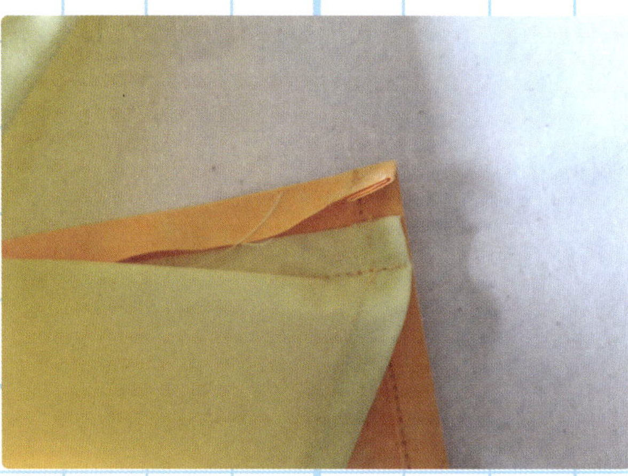

(4) Iron the seam.

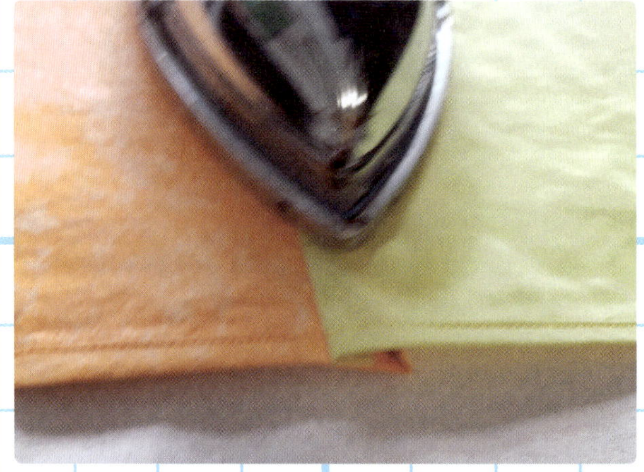

(5) On the front side, stitch at 2mm from the
border of the fold.

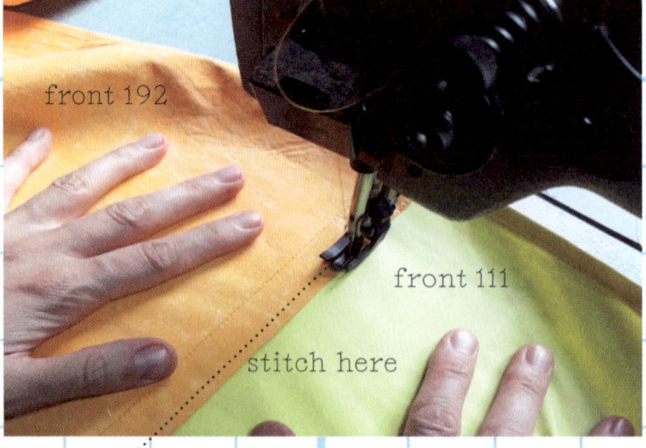

2.3. assemble 111 + 192

(1) On the right side of piece 192: fold and steam
iron 1 cm to the backside. On the left side of piece
111: fold and steam iron 1cm to the front side. If
necessary, draw guide lines on the fabric (e.g. at
20mm).
Place piece 192 on the table, backside facing
up. Place piece 111, front side facing up. Both
backsides of the fabric face towards each other.

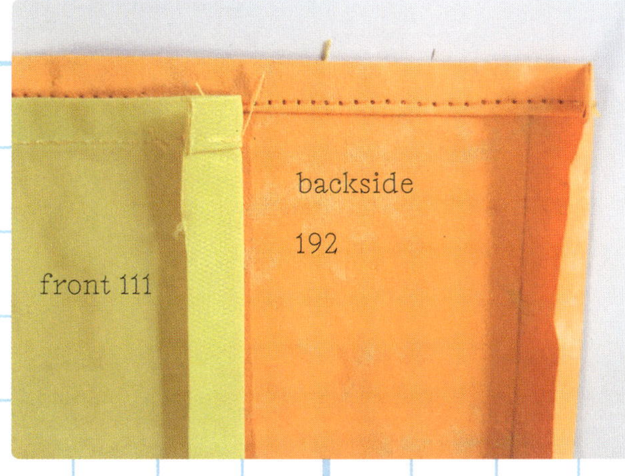

(2) Unfold edge of piece 111 and place it border
to border to the folded edge of piece 192. Pin and
stitch both pieces together in the folding line
of piece 111 (= 20mm from the edge). Make sure
to use the correct colors for the top and bottom
threads in the machine.

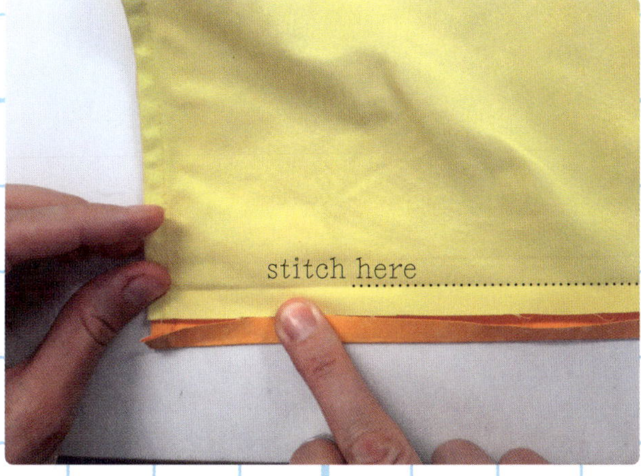

2.5 assemble all pieces

(1) (2) Place piece 192/111 on the table, backside facing up.
Fold piece 206 in half and place it on top of piece 192. The free edges slide under the 40mm border of 192.
Then bend piece 192/111 and slide it via the underside in between the 2 layers of piece 206. The free edge of 111 moves along under the 40mm border of 192.

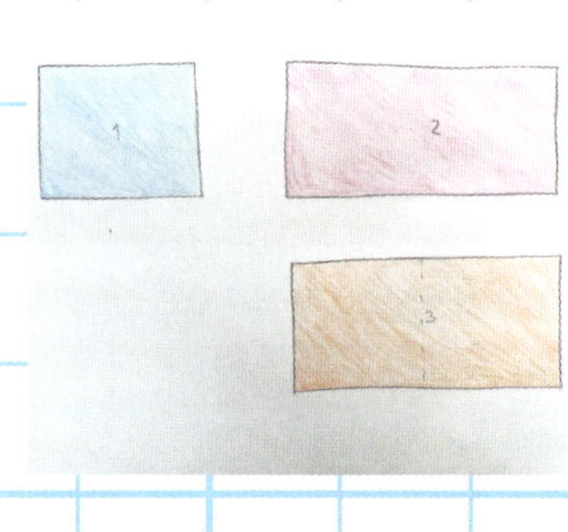

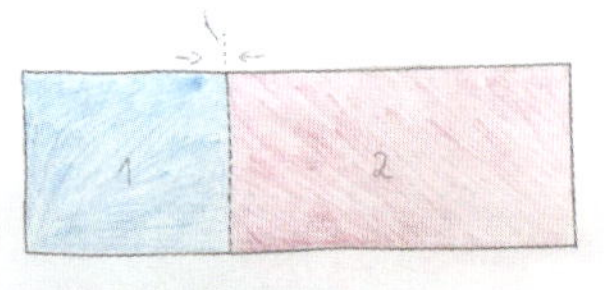

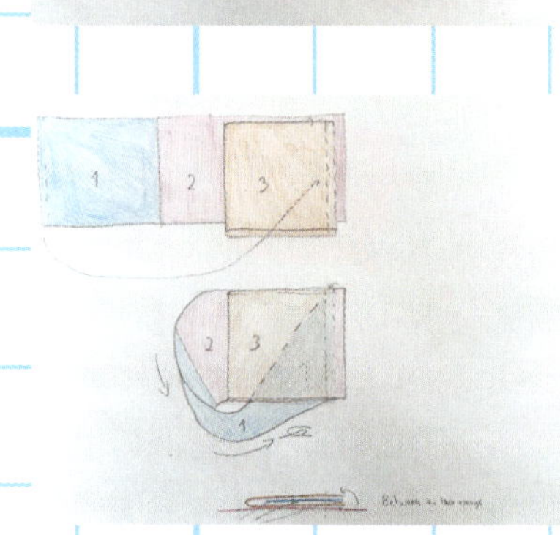

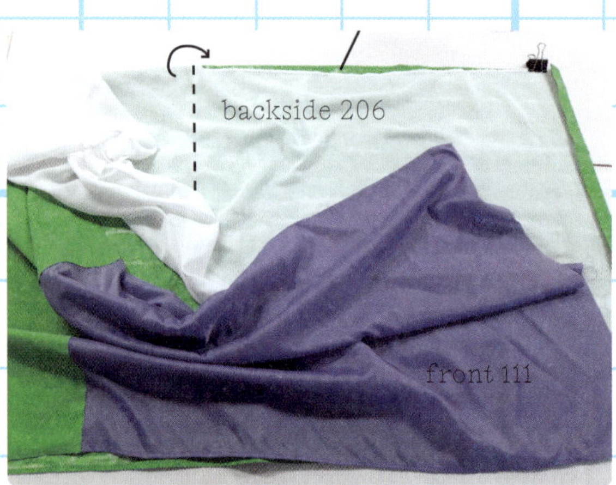

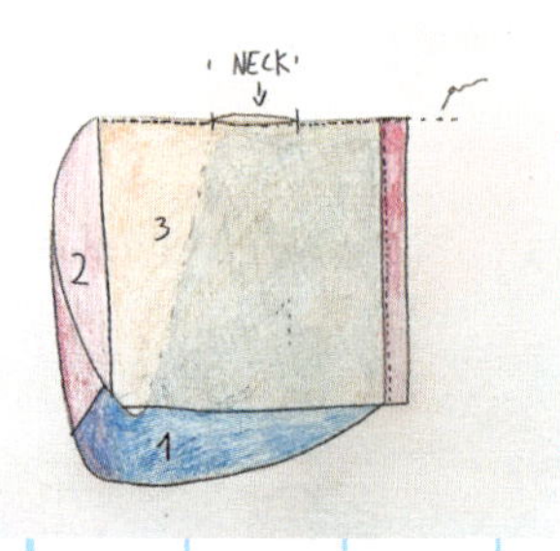

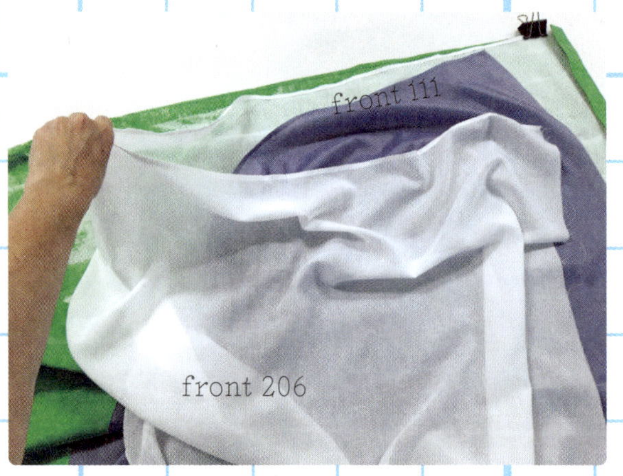

2.4 preparing border 192

(1) (2) (3) Place piece 192 (attached to piece 111) with front side down on the table. Fold 2 x 40mm to the backside of the fabric. Steam iron the folds to get solid fold lines. If necessary, draw guide lines on the fabric (e.g. at 80mm).

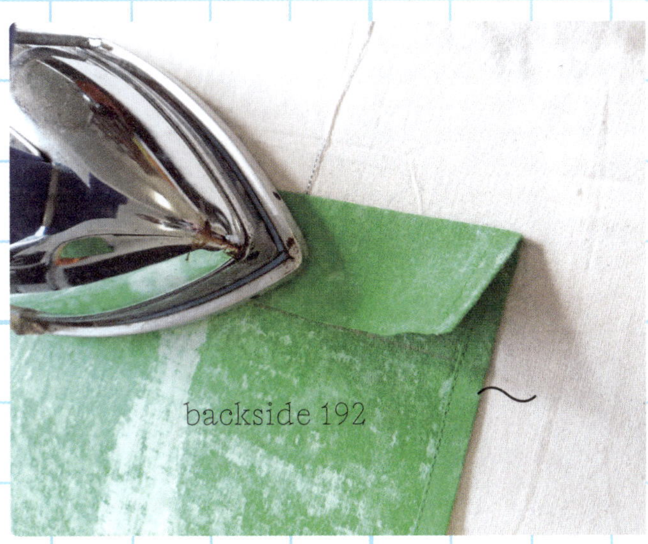

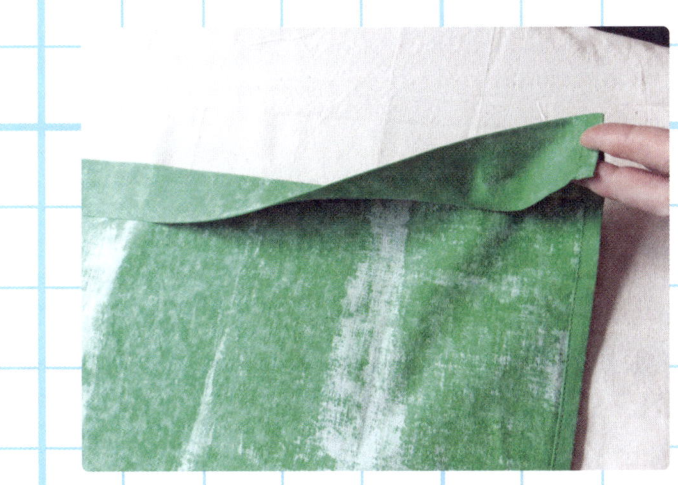

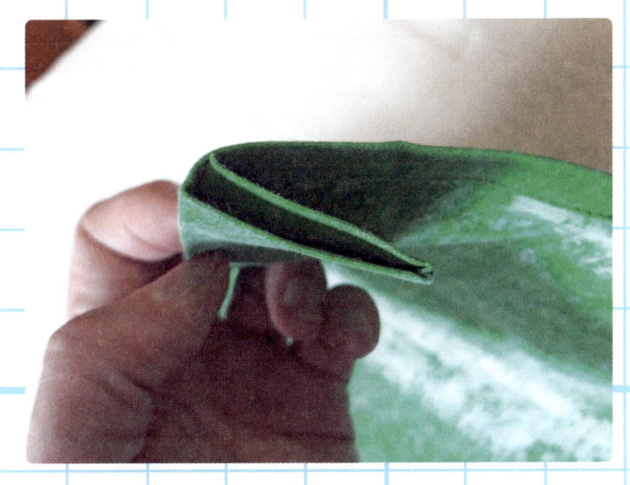

(6) Stitch on the edge.

(7) Result

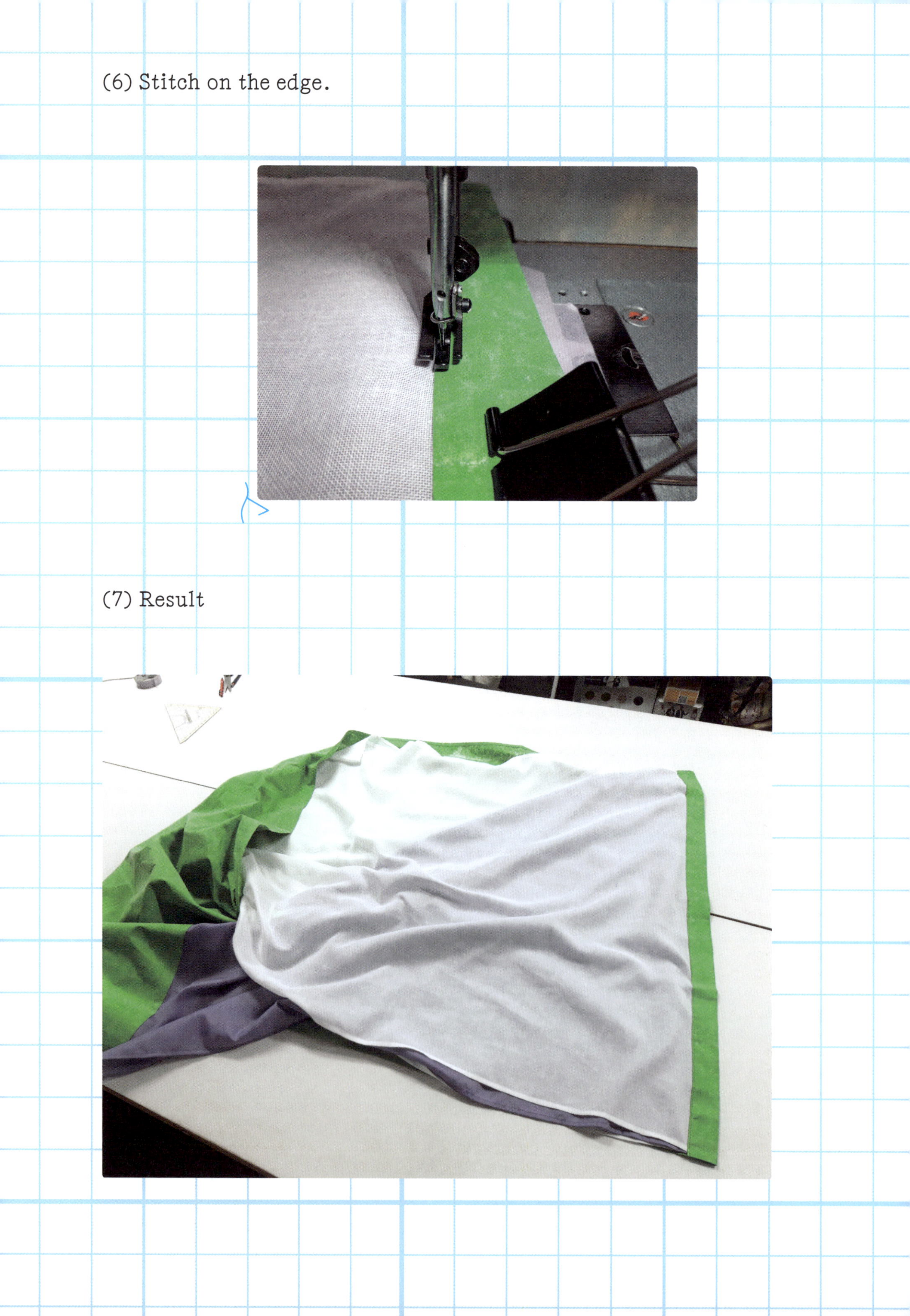

(3) Align the 3 edges of the double folded piece
206 with 111 in between and place them against
the inner fold of the 40mm border of 192.

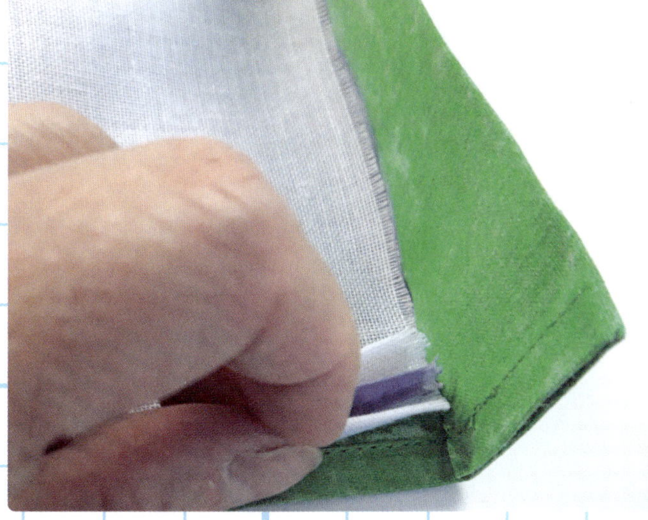

(4) Close the prefolded 40 mm border of 192

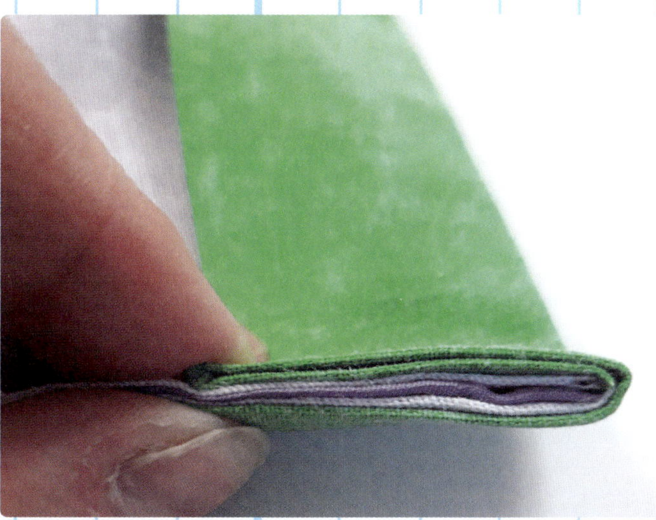

(5) Pin or clip the edge so that the different layers
remain properly in place while sewing.

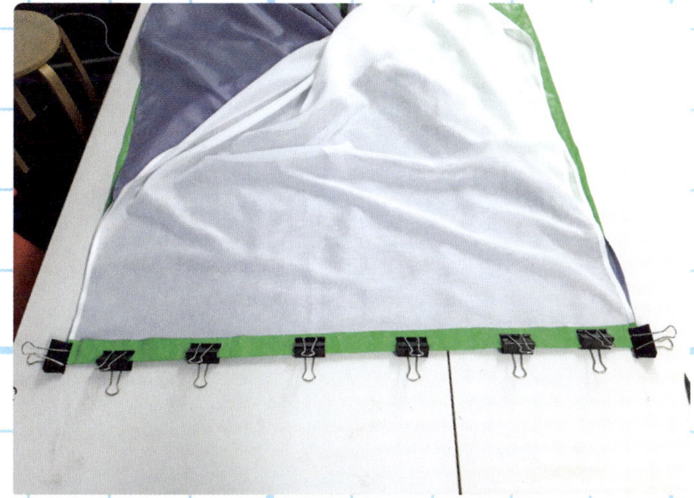

2.7 assembling shoulders

(1) Part 1 of the shoulders = from the inside edge
of the 40 mm border of piece 192 up to the left
side of the neckline opening.
All 4 layers of fabric (192 + 206/part 1 + 111 + 206/
part 2) are gathered together, overlapping the
edges of the upper hems.
Sew close to the edge. (Together with the hem
stitch you see 2 stitching lines.)

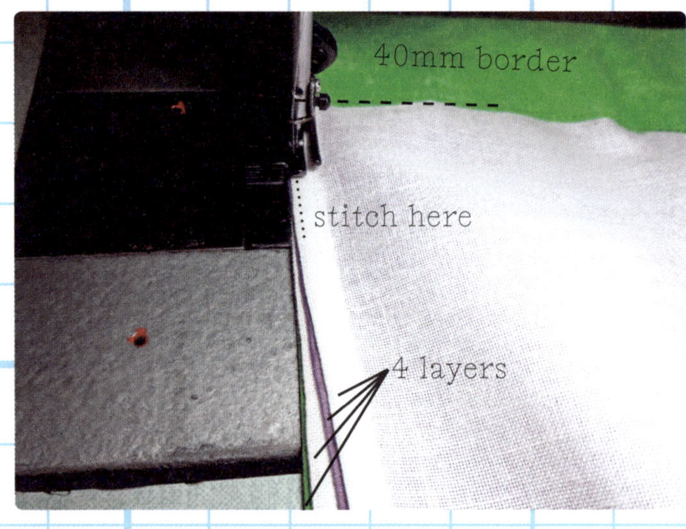

(2) When you get to the left side of the neck
opening: sew a small rectangle and its diagonals
to make a solid point.

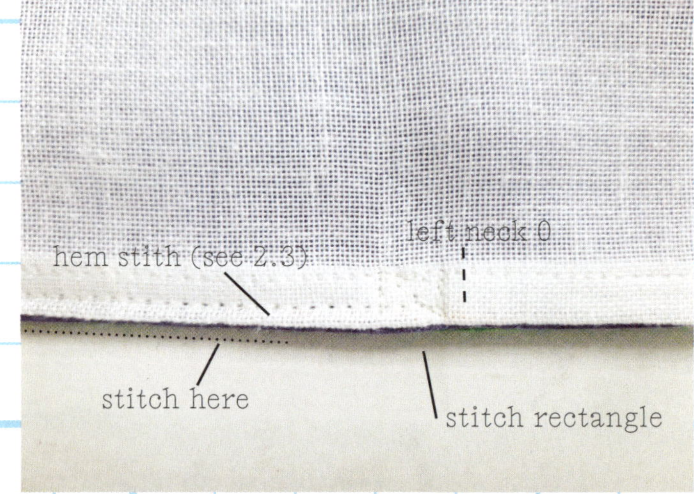

2.6 preparing shoulders

(1) Measure and pin the center of the neck
opening = 495mm from the inner edge of the
40mm border of piece 192.

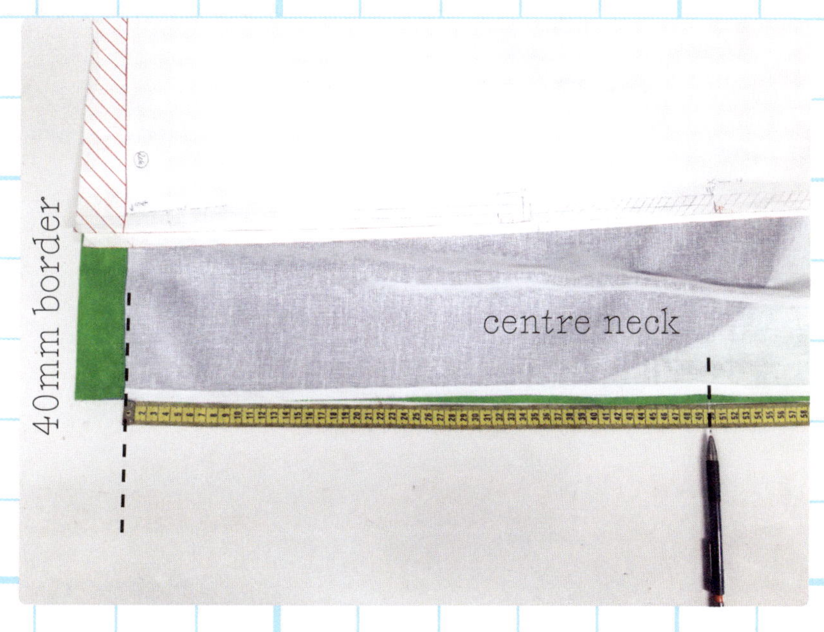

(2) Measure and pin the opening from the center
of the neck = 180mm to the left and right.

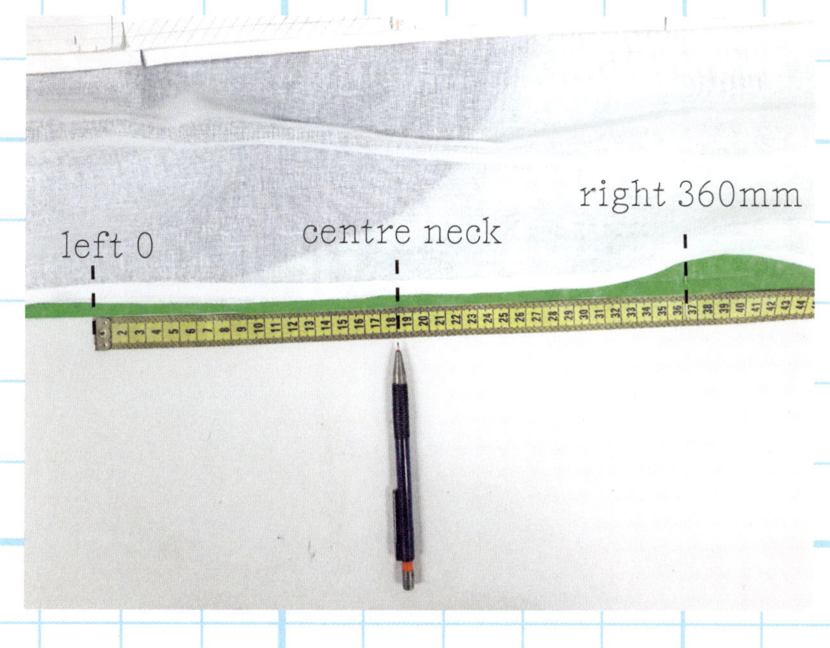

(5) Part 3 of the shoulders = from the right side
of the neckline opening up to the middle folding
line of piece 206.
Three layers of fabric (192 + 206/part 1 + 206/
part 2) are joined together, overlapping the edges
of the upper hems.

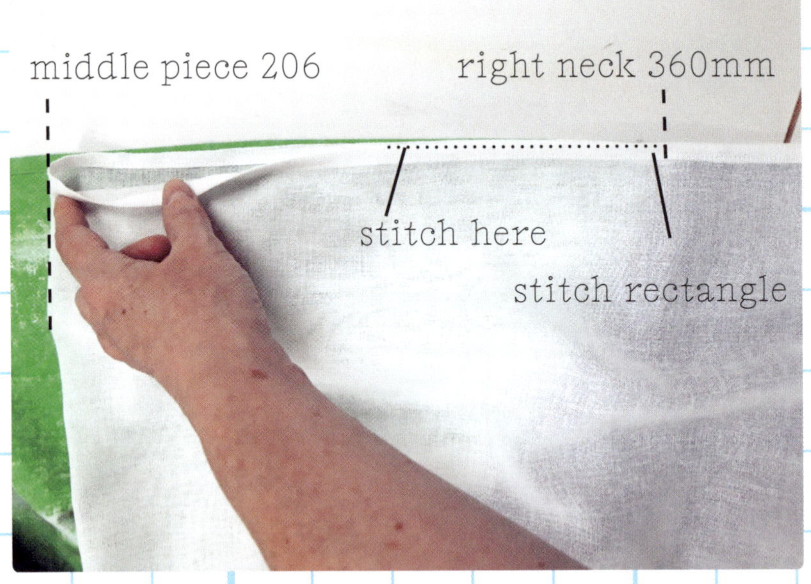

(6) Fold piece 111 aside and sew close to the edge.
At the right side of the neckline opening: start
by sewing a small rectangle and the diagonals to
make a solid point.

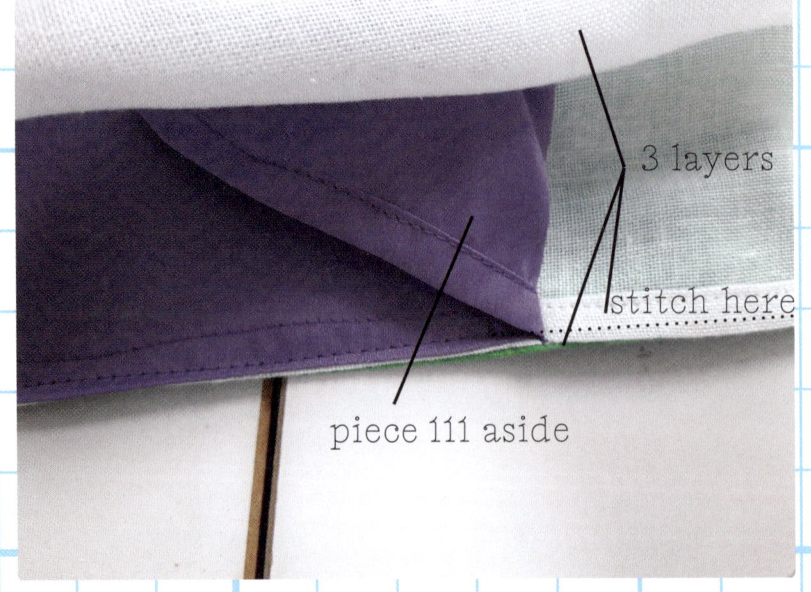

(3) Part 2 of the shoulders = neck opening from
the left to the right marking point.
Three layers of fabric (192 + 206/part 1 + 111)
are joined together, overlapping the edges of the
upper hems.
Fold piece 206/part 2 aside and sew close to the
edge.

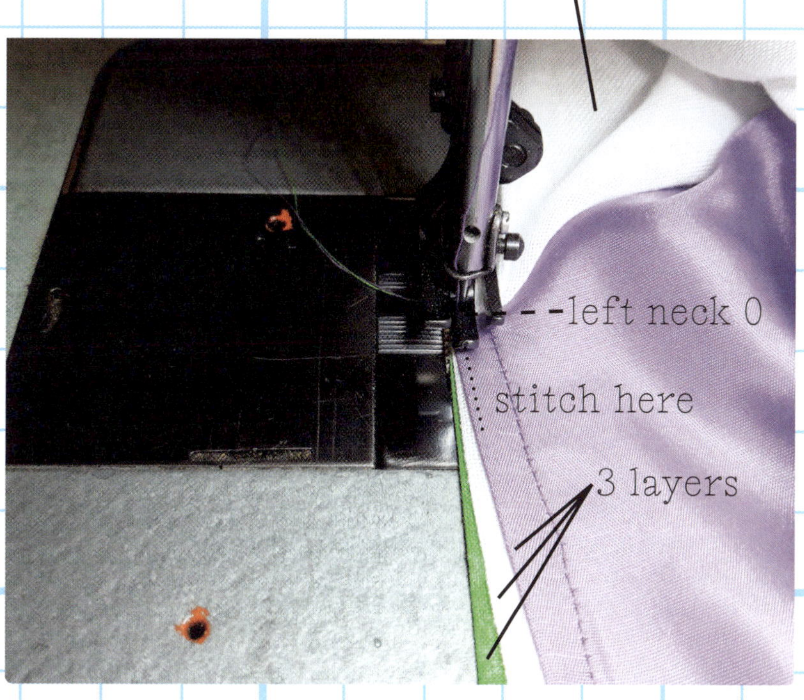

(4) Start and finish by sewing a small rectangle
and the diagonals to make solid points.

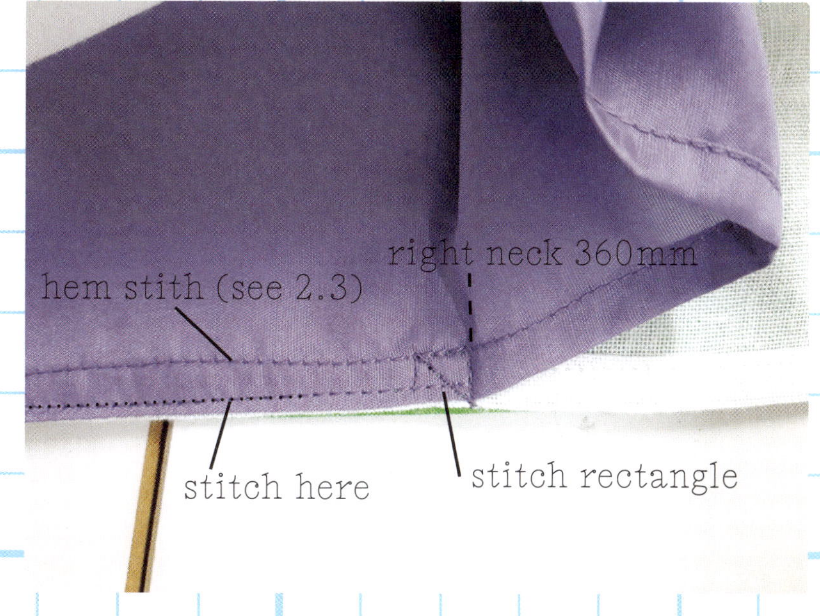

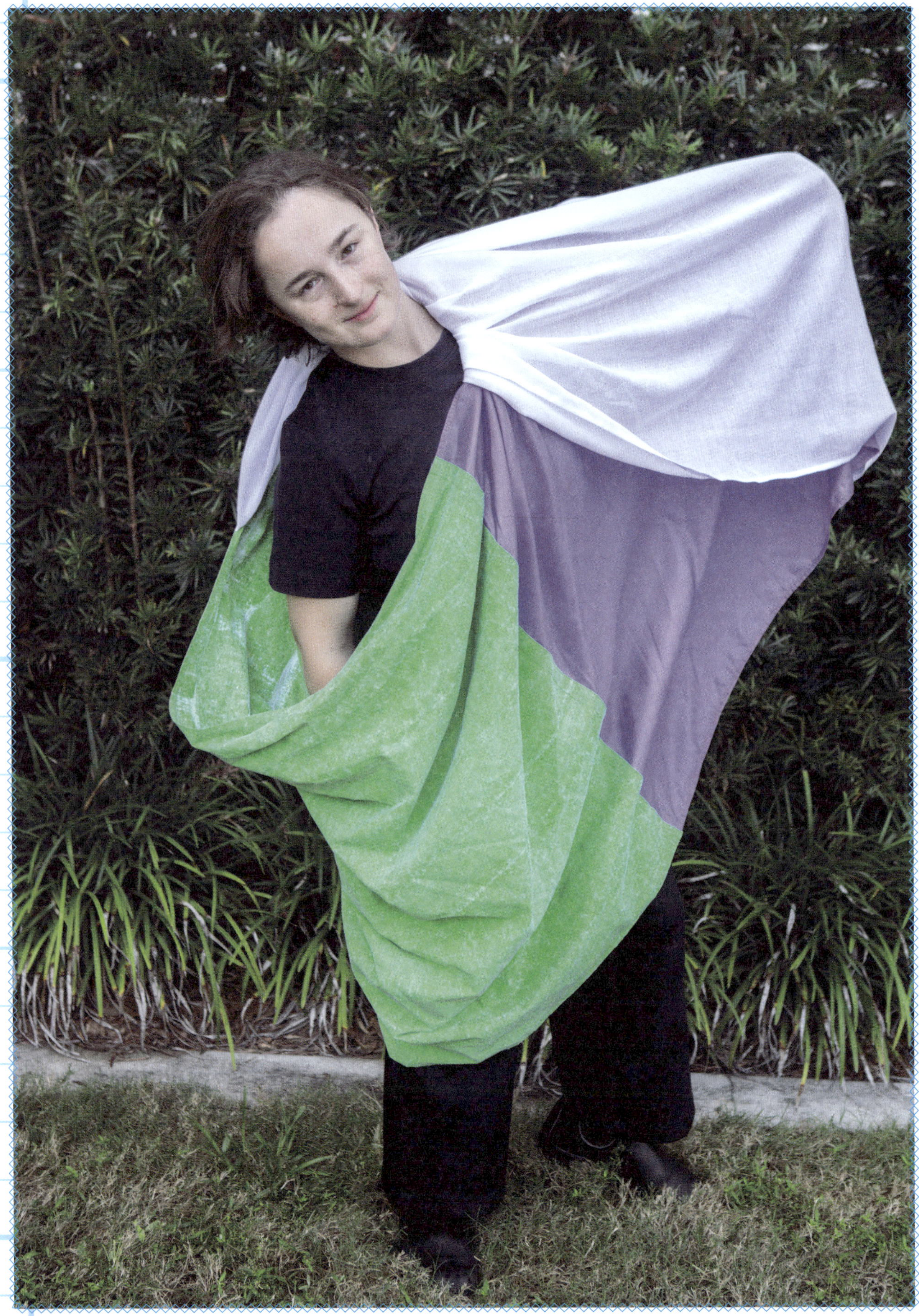

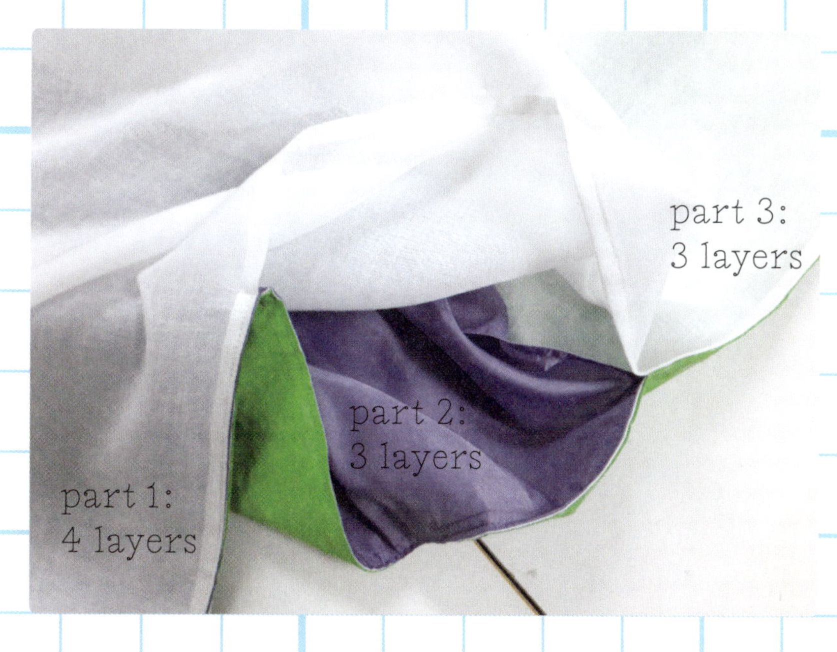

(8) At the end of the shoulder = the middle
folding line of piece 206: NO rectangle.

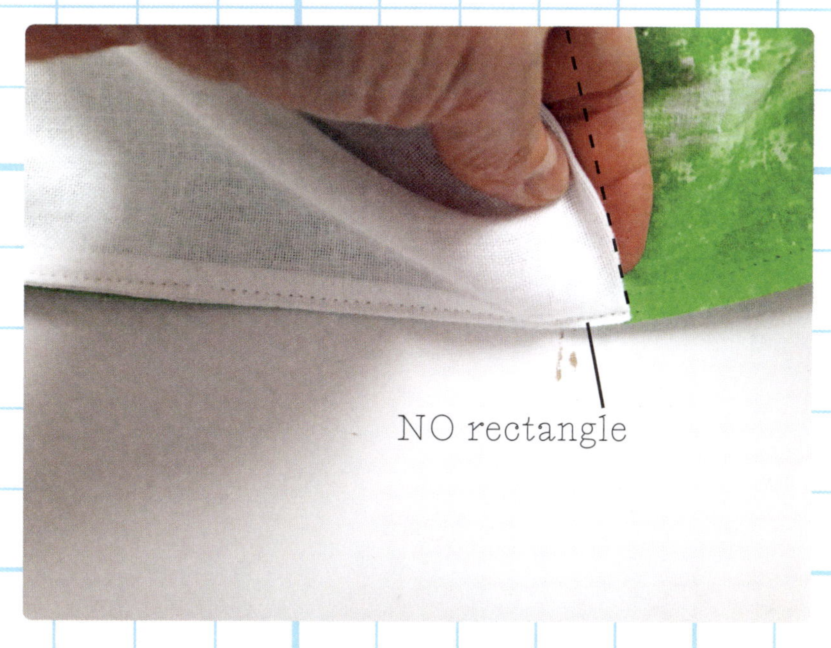

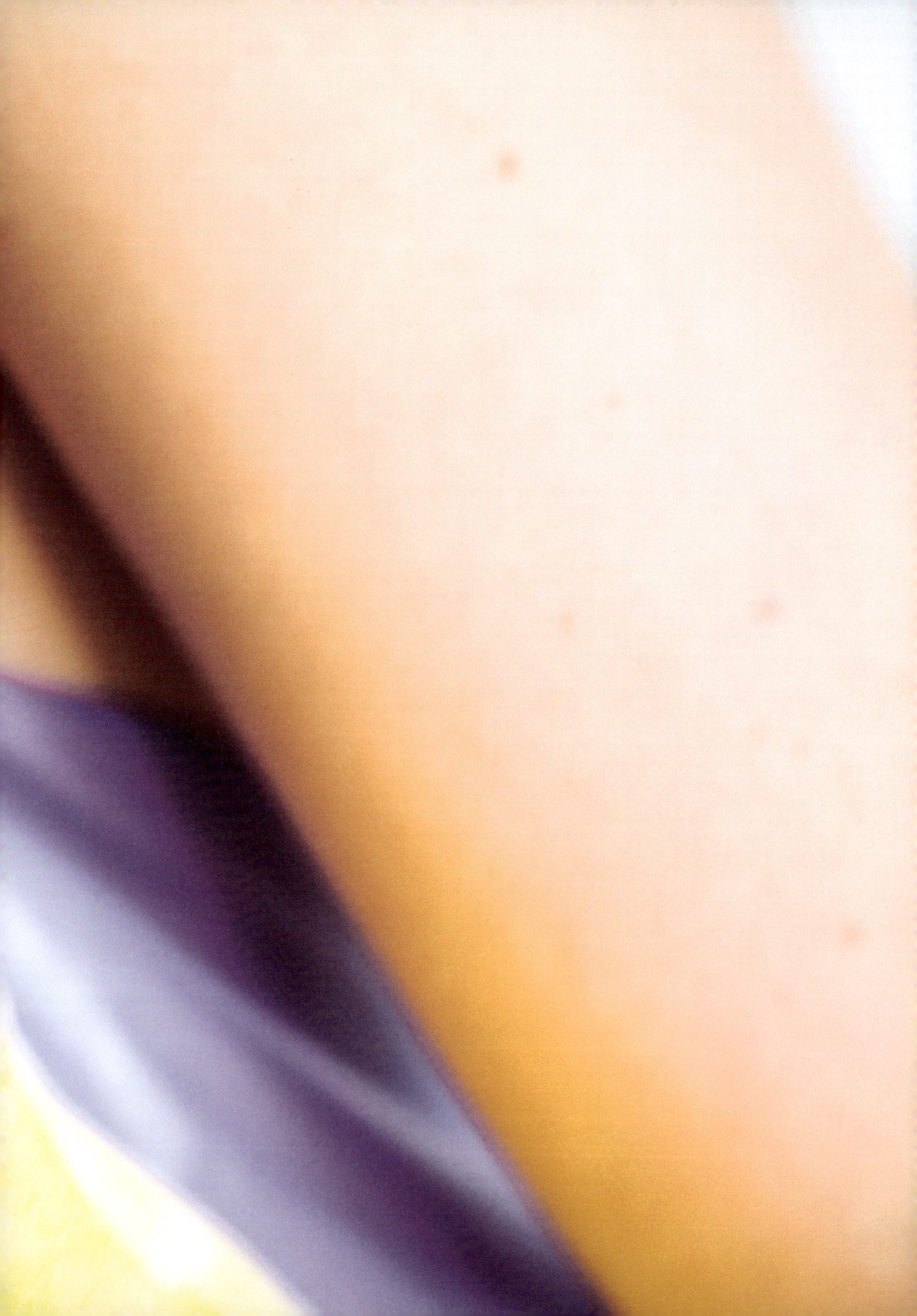

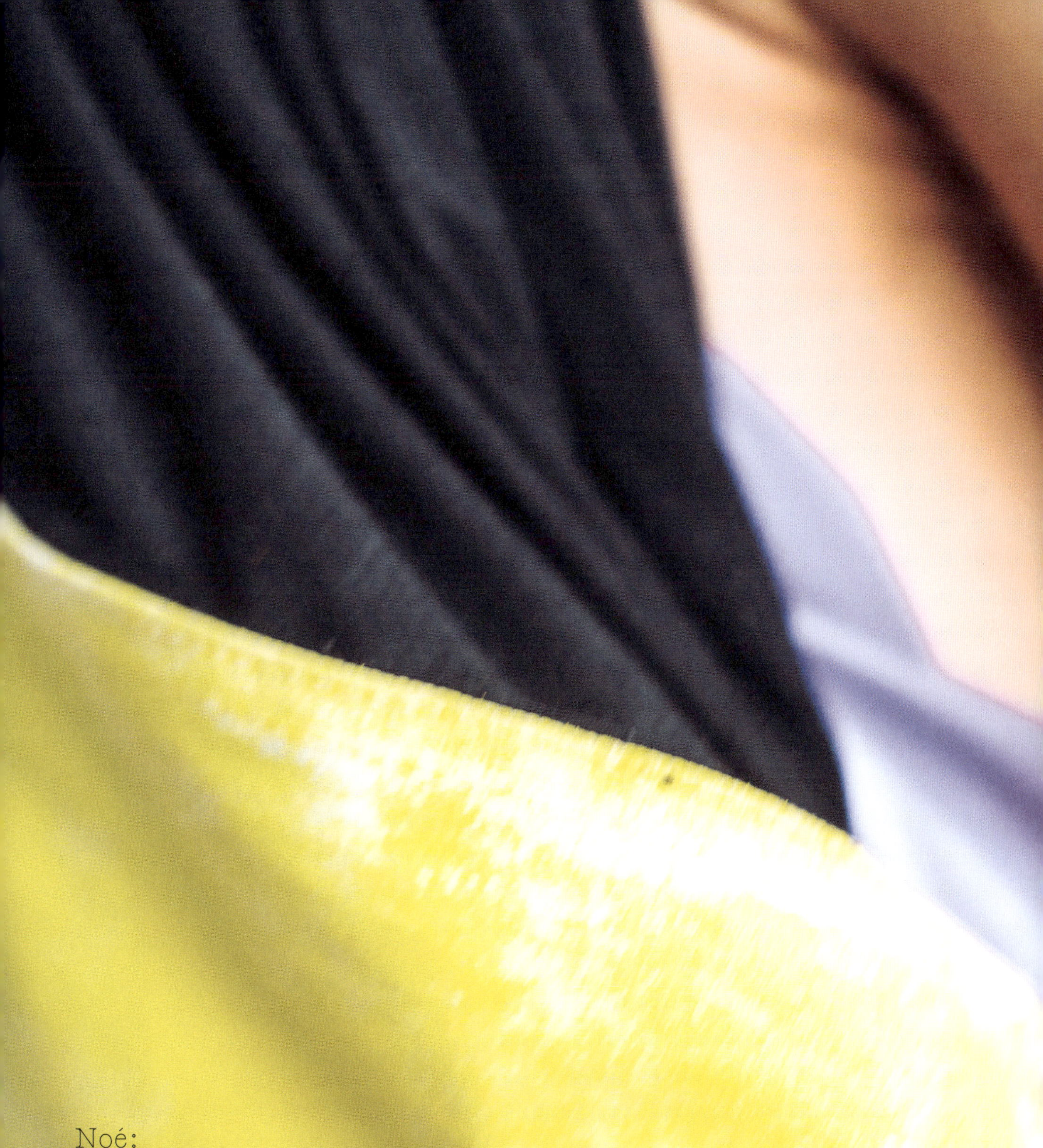

Noé:

I truly enjoyed wearing and embracing this non-binary costume. Although wearing it in public wasn't easy, the teamwork gave me confidence, and I felt proud to be part of this group. The way the fabric moved against my skin, its sensuality, made the experience even more intimate, almost as if the costume was an extension of myself.

Another question I have is: To what extent can art create the conditions to experience a message? *To explore this, I have worked on activating my artworks, or "explorations." For several pieces, I've asked a museum's mediation team to activate them through a script involving movement and text. Unlike many archival practices where the installation is the endpoint, I consider it the starting point . The mediated information can transcend mere data, involving sound, material properties, or composition. This activation, through text and tactile manipulation by a mediator, introduces another way of "being with" the work. In these moments, the work exists, meaning it has duration and plays between moments of appearance (when activated) and disappearance (when not activat-* ed). *The question* "When is art?" *lies at the heart of my* research project, "The Archive of Disappearance".

Your approach to making the public a participant inspired my recent work, as a mediation team isn't always available in every context. My work "I am I," a portrait of two friends based on their information and gender theory, is activated by the friends themselves. Their fluid portrait becomes an artwork through their activation, changing with each public interaction. Finally, you described your artworks as living entities that can evolve. Irène Small notes that your work rejects discrete objects in favor of experiential, environmental, and informational works. Your concern with aesthetic, social, and psychic emancipation critiques institutional protocols, shifting the focus from authorial creation to the viewer's reception, interpretation, and use of art. I wonder about the relationship between the form, material, and shape of the different Parangolés *and the audience's experience of them. This remains a mystery to me and, I suspect, will continue to be an open question.*

LDB[+]

Letter t° Hélio Oiticica!

Dear Hélio,

Even though you are no longer with us, I address this letter to you. Over the past year, engaging with your work has been a revelation for me. I wish I could discuss some topics with you that I believe are essential for the development of any artistic practice today.

I have been exploring ways to engage with art more holistically, beyond mere intellectual observation. Some visitors to my installations feel that my work assumes prior knowledge of certain architectural, art historical, or theoretical references, which is necessary to fully 'understand' it. I empathize with this critique, as it applies to many contemporary art practices situated within what Hal Foster calls the "archival impulse" or Nicolas Bourriaud describes as "post-production."

The first question I would ask your audience is: What kind of experience does your art create? This concern permeated your artistic practice and grew stronger over time, eventually becoming the core reason for your art's existence.
The Parangolés are, for me, the most inspiring and enigmatic part of your work. These capes, which the public can wear and dance with, express ideas about color and convey political statements. Through this interaction, visitors experience the deintellectualization of art you aimed for, evoking an institutional critique you articulated in "The World as Museum." The Parangolés delve into the meaning of being colored. When one wears a Parangolé and dances, they experience what I would call a 'moment of getting lost', or as you put it, the creation of one's own time and freedom. It highlights the gaze at the other and the issue of being different. This moment of being lost, of experiencing another time and place, of creating the context and meaning of the work, is what you call "Creleisure" (creation and leisure). This concept currently interests me in my own practice.

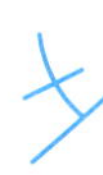

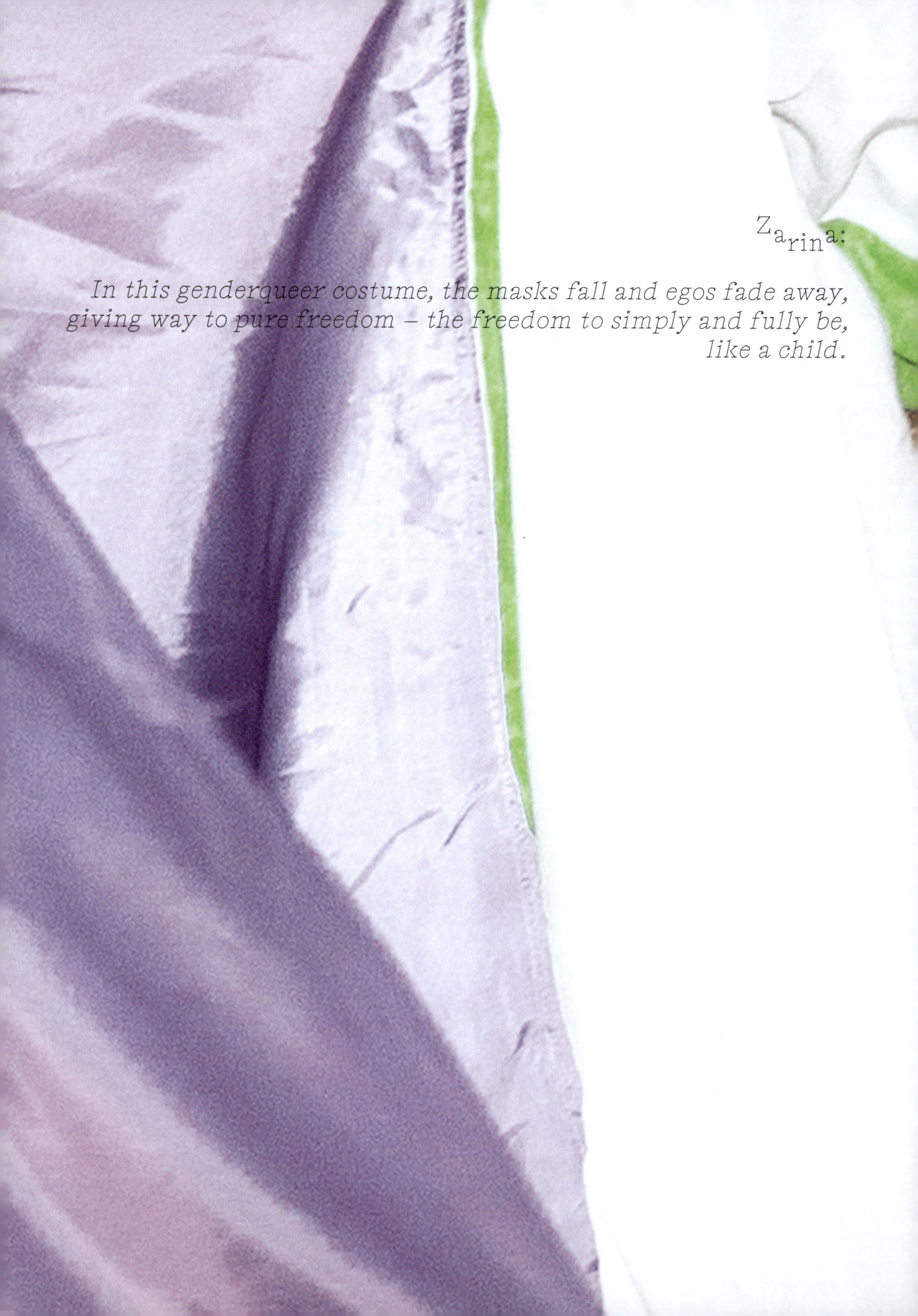

Zarina:

In this genderqueer costume, the masks fall and egos fade away,
giving way to pure freedom – the freedom to simply and fully be,
like a child.

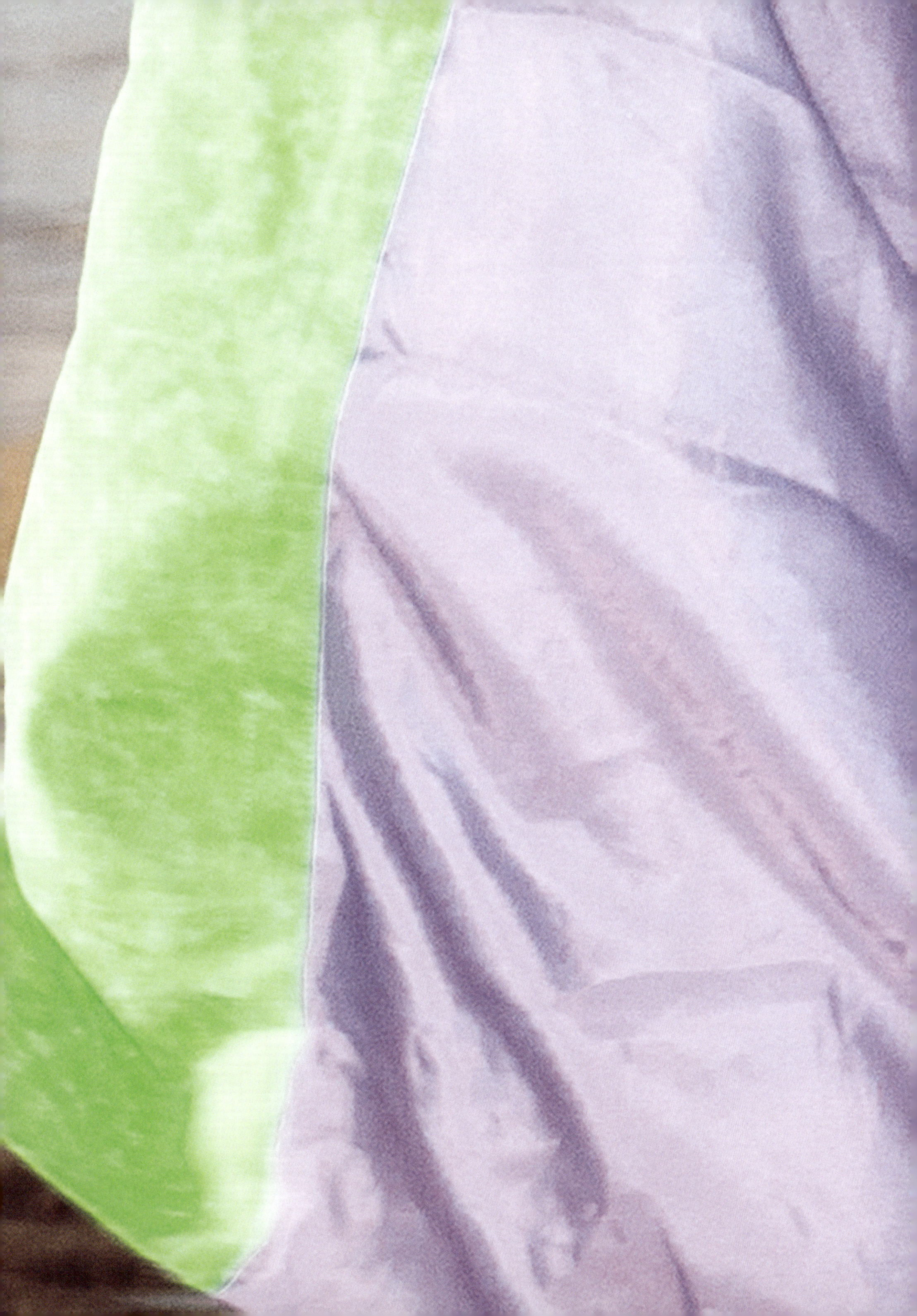

a manual for painting textile

| Materials: | o | natural fiber fabric of the appropriate size |
| | o | paint |

Tools:	o	large brush
	o	paint receptacle
	o	waterproof hard surface
	o	weights (brick, wood, etc.)
	o	iron
	o	protective cloth
	o	washing machine
	o	drying rack or stretched rope

Queering Oiticica

In revisiting Hélio Oiticica's *Parangolé Capa 21,* one question remains unresolved: how did Oiticica select the colours, fabrics, and materials for his original work? This detail, crucial to faithfully reproducing the *Parangolé* decades later, lacks a clear historical answer. However, the question finds resolution by contextualizing the project in the present.

Oiticica, who was queer himself, frequently sought refuge in the favelas, spaces where he could freely explore and express his identity. In this spirit, the contemporary reinterpretation of the Parangolé embraces a similar ethos. Rather than replicating the exact materials and colours of Oiticica's time, the new version allows participants to express their own queer and gender identities by choosing colours from the gender flags that represent them.

As an example of this approach, LDB⁺ produced seven sample *Parangolés* inspired by different gender and queer flag combinations. However, during the production of these examples, several challenges arose.

Finding fabrics in the exact colours of the flags proved difficult, prompting Studio LDB⁺ to begin painting the fabrics themselves, which eventually led to the creation of a detailed fabric-painting manual.

Additionally, combining more than three colours within costumes made from only three pieces of fabric presented another obstacle. This challenge was solved by painting both sides of the fabric, enabling the use of a broader colour palette and allowing for greater expression through the interplay of hues.

This adaptation honours Oiticica's original vision of personal and social expression, while grounding it in a modern context that celebrates the diversity of identity through artistic creation and self-representation.

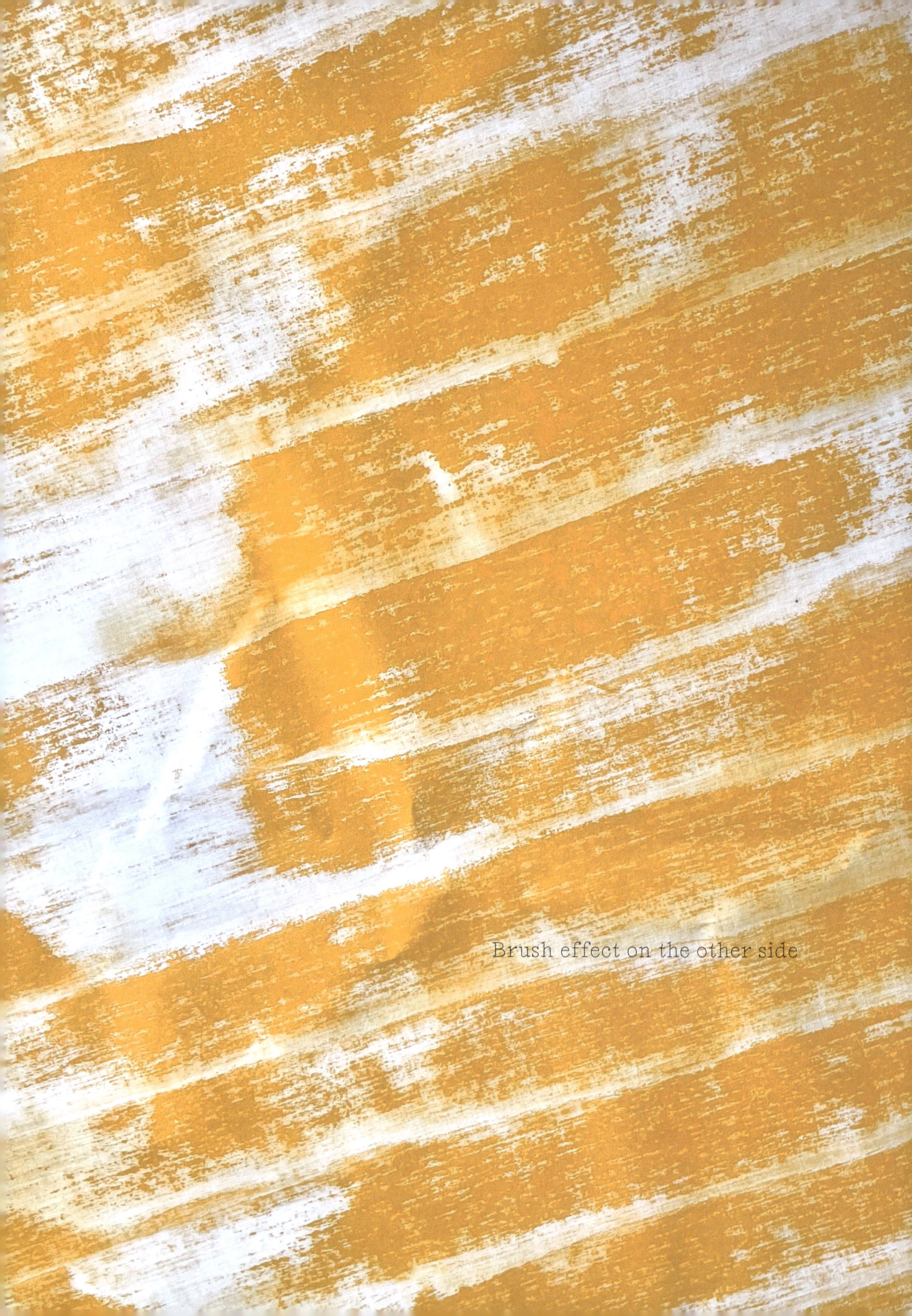
Brush effect on the other side

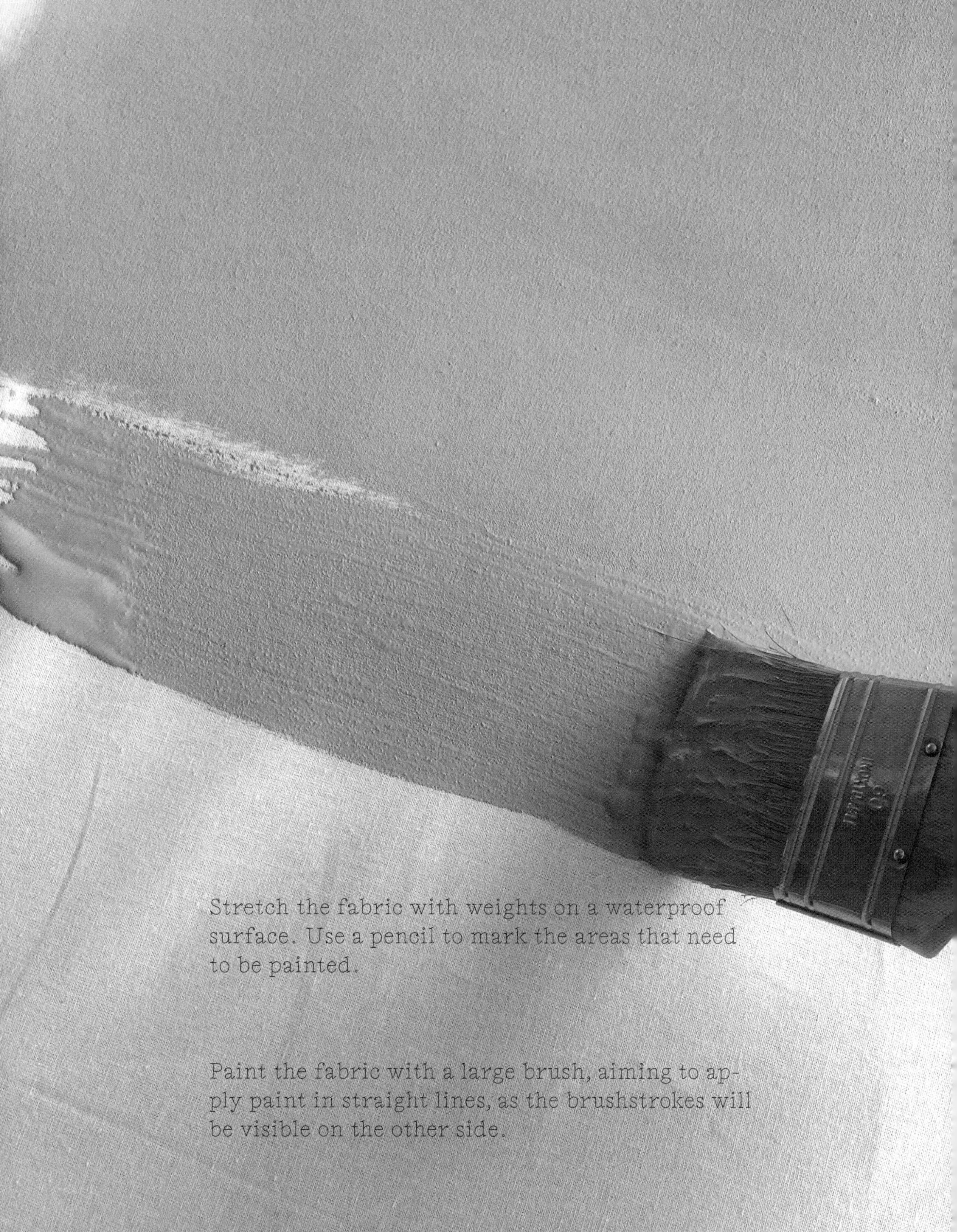

Stretch the fabric with weights on a waterproof
surface. Use a pencil to mark the areas that need
to be painted.

Paint the fabric with a large brush, aiming to apply paint in straight lines, as the brushstrokes will
be visible on the other side.

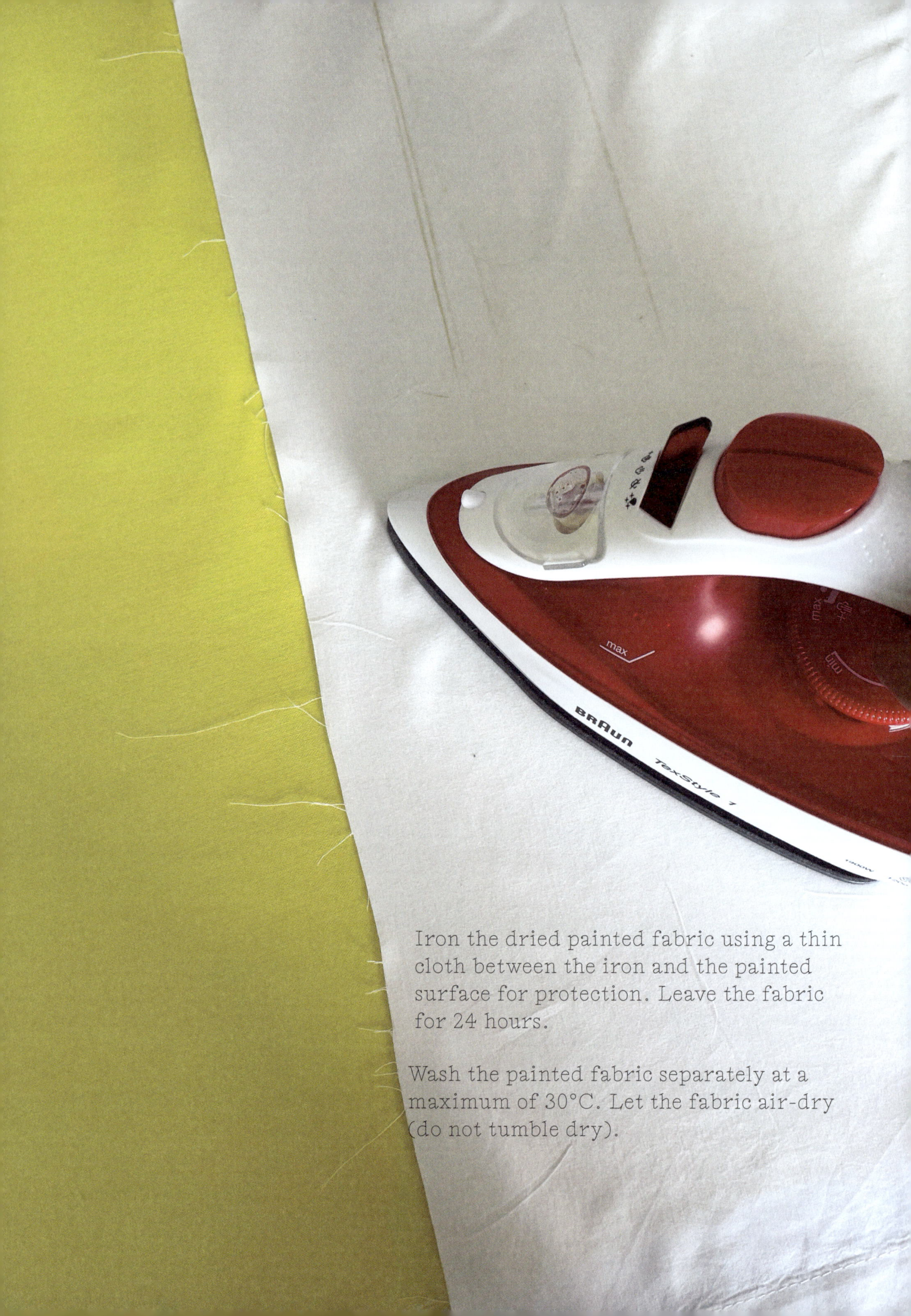

Iron the dried painted fabric using a thin
cloth between the iron and the painted
surface for protection. Leave the fabric
for 24 hours.

Wash the painted fabric separately at a
maximum of 30°C. Let the fabric air-dry
(do not tumble dry).

Allow the fabric and paint to dry for 24 hours on the waterproof surface.

If the fabric needs to be painted in two different colors, paint the other side while it's on the water-proof surface and let the paint dry.

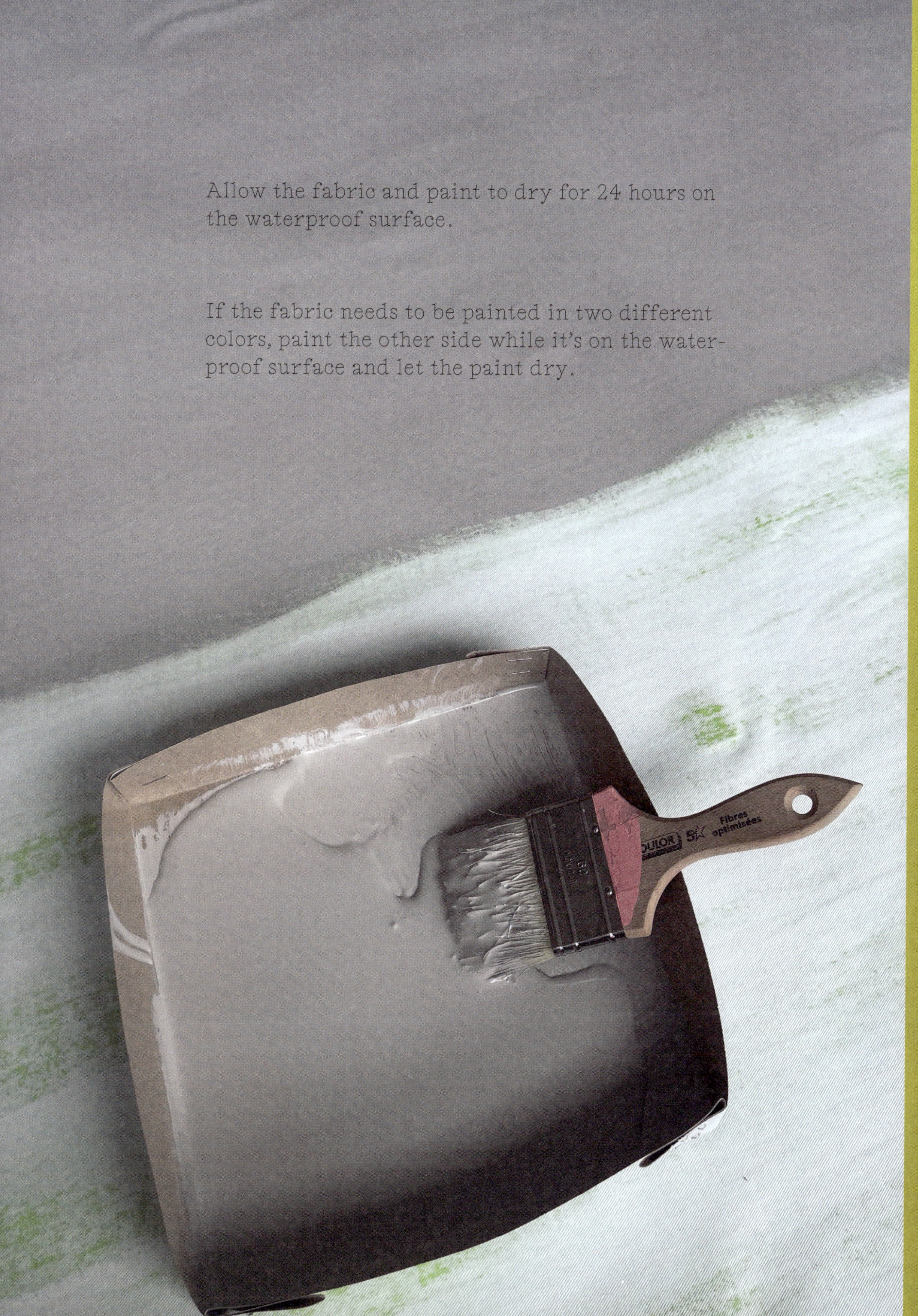

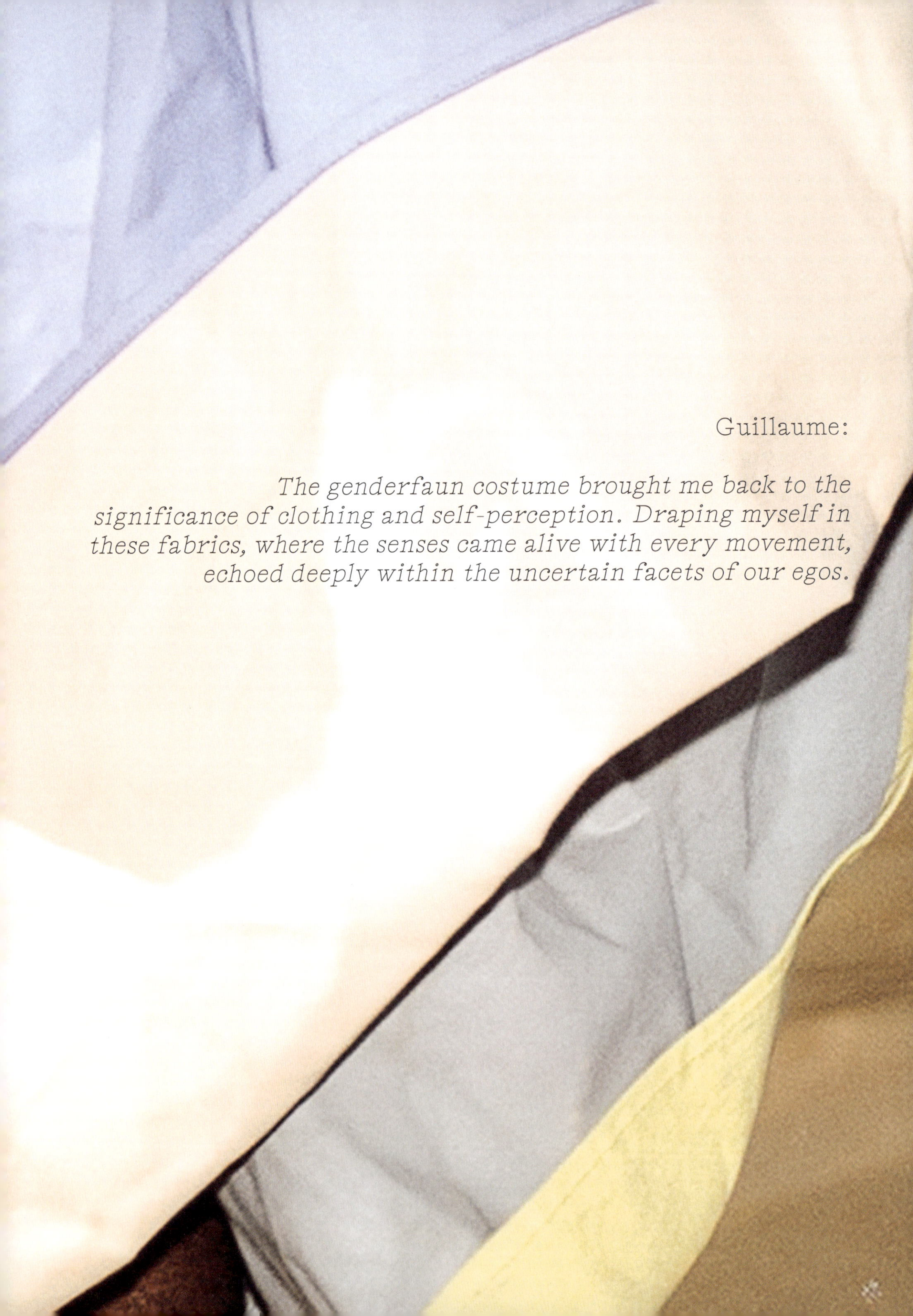
Guillaume:

The genderfaun costume brought me back to the significance of clothing and self-perception. Draping myself in these fabrics, where the senses came alive with every movement, echoed deeply within the uncertain facets of our egos.

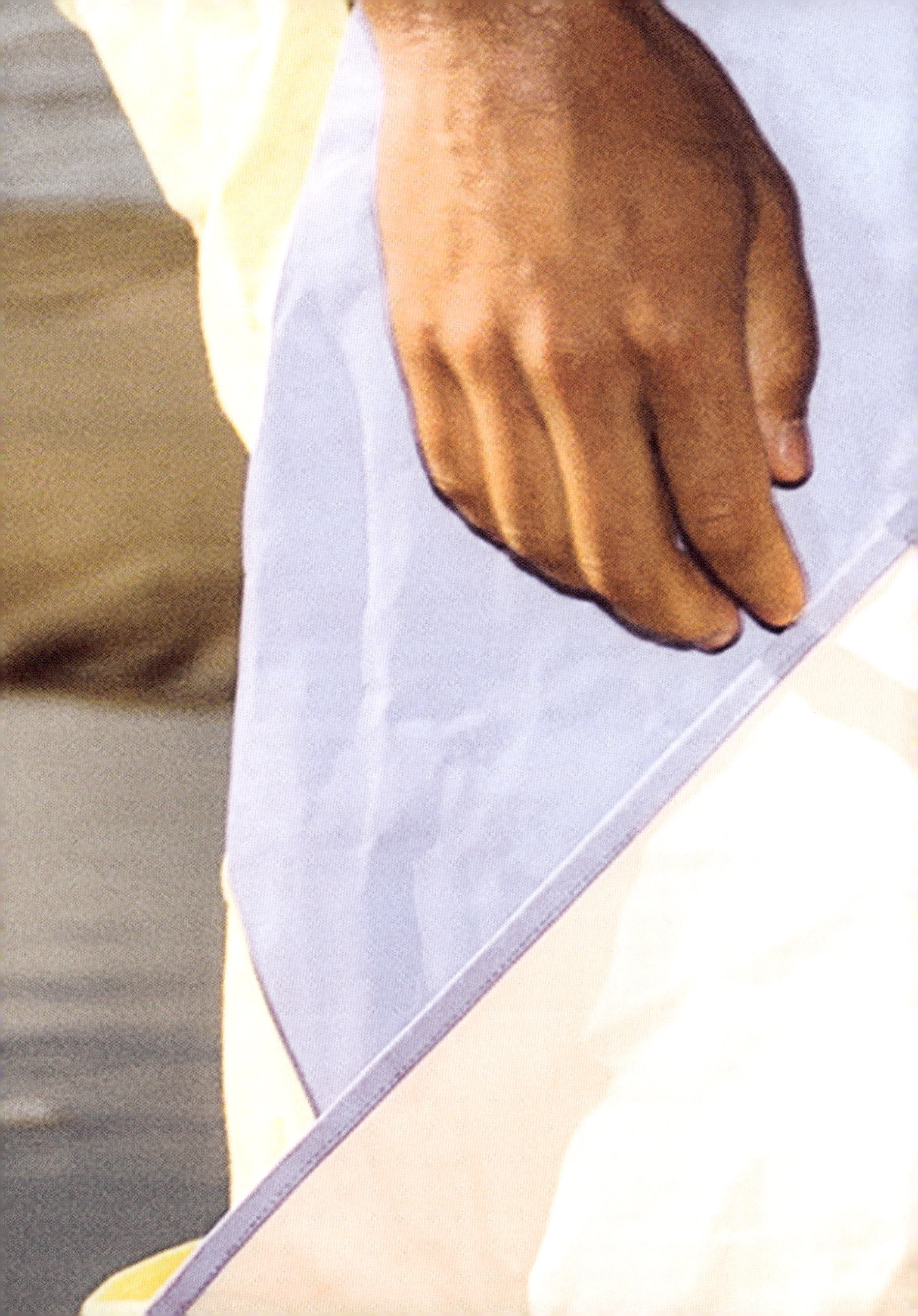

Genderqueer

A genderqueer person does not adhere to traditional gender norms but identifies as neither, both, or a combination of male and female genders. The term *genderqueer* is sometimes used interchangeably with *non-binary*. This flag is one of the most commonly used symbols within the non-binary community.

The genderqueer flag consists of green, white, and purple. Green represents non-binary identities, white symbolizes the presence or absence of gender, and purple stands for a blend of both masculine and feminine genders.

Colors and fabric used:

Couleur : mauve
Dimension : 111 x 97,6 cm
Textile : coton

Couleur : blanc
Dimension : 206 x 97,6 cm
Textile : coton opaque

Couleur : vert
Dimension : 192 x 99,2 cm
Textile : synthétique

Agender

The term *agender* refers to the absence of gender. It is often described as being non-gendered or genderless. There can be some overlap with those who identify as *neutral*, individuals who experience a gender identity that is neither male nor female.

In the agender pride flag, both black and white symbolize the complete absence of gender. Grey represents a partial or semi-genderless state, while green signifies non-binary gender identities, as it is the opposite of purple (which traditionally blends red and blue, colors often associated with binary gender identities).

Colors and fabric used:

Couleur : noir
Dimension : 206 x 97,6 cm
Textile : Fluide synthétique

Couleur : gris
Dimension : 206 x 97,6 cm
Textile : syn- thétique
(style imper- méable)

Couleur : blanc
Dimension : 111 x 97,6 cm
Textile : coton

Couleur : vert clair
Dimension : 192 x 99,7 cm
Textile : coton épais

Transgender

Transgender, or trans, is a broad term that covers all gender identities or expressions that defy or go beyond society's conventional ideas of gender.

Being trans generally means identifying with a gender different from the one assigned at birth. While "transgender" is often associated with binary gender identities—such as transgender women (assigned male at birth but identifying as female) and transgender men (assigned female at birth but identifying as male)—this view is incomplete. The transgender umbrella also includes individuals with nonbinary gender identities, though not all nonbinary people see themselves as transgender.

The transgender flag features three colors: blue, pink, and white. The light blue represents the traditional color for boys, pink symbolizes the traditional color for girls, and white stands for those who are nonbinary, gender nonconforming, or transitioning.

Colors and fabric used:

Couleur : bleu
Dimension : 206 x 97,6 cm
Textile : coton

Couleur : blanc
Dimension : 111 x 97,6 cm
Textile : coton léger

Couleur : rose
Dimension : 192 x 99,2 cm
Textile : synthétique

Maverique

Maverique is a non-binary gender identity defined by a strong and distinct sense of gender that is completely independent of traditional concepts like male, female, or neutral. Unlike some non-binary identities that may involve an absence of gender or a lack of concern about gender, maverique is characterized by a clear and unique gender experience.

However, maveriques can also identify as multigender, meaning they may experience other genders in addition to their maverique identity, which could relate to maleness, femaleness, or neutrality.

The maverique flag features three colors: yellow, symbolizing autonomy and independence from traditional gender identities; white, representing inner clarity and the distinct sense of self; and orange, which stands for the unique and vibrant sense of gender experienced by maveriques, independent of male, female, or neutral identities.

Colors and fabric used:

Couleur : jaune
Dimension : 111 x 97,6 cm
Textile : synthétique fluide

Couleur : blanc
Dimension : 206 x 97,6 cm
Textile : synthétique transparent

Couleur : orange
Dimension : 192 x 99,2 cm
Textile : coton ou synthétique mat, peinture orange

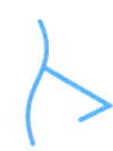

Non-binary

Non-binary is a broad umbrella term for individuals who do not conform to the traditional binary gender structure of male and female. While many non-binary identities have their own specific terms, feelings, and flags, some individuals prefer to use the term non-binary to describe their gender experience without adopting a more specific label.

The non-binary flag features four colors: yellow, white, purple, and black. This flag is one of the most commonly recognized symbols within the non-binary community.
In this flag, yellow represents non-masculine and non-feminine genders; white signifies all genders; purple embodies a blend of masculine and feminine identities; and black stands for non-genders. Together, these colors reflect the diverse spectrum of non-binary identities.

Colors and fabric used:

Couleur : Jaune
Dimension : 206 x 97,6 cm
Textile : Synthétique (kway)

Couleur : Blanc
Dimension : 111 x 97,6 cm
Textile : Tulle

Couleur : Mauve
Dimension : 192 x 99,2 cm
Textile : Coton

Couleur : Noir
Dimension : 192 x 99,2 cm
Textile : Synthétique fluide

Genderflux

Genderflux is a gender identity characterized by varying intensities over time. It can fall under the umbrellas of genderfluidity, non-binary, and transgender identities. Some individuals conceptualize genderflux as a fluid movement between an agender identity and one or more distinct gender identities. Another way to think about it is to envision the intensity of one or more gender identities on a scale from 0% to 100%. As one person described it: "The idea is that my gender, and by extension my presentation, is sometimes a really, really loud version of itself and sometimes it's quiet, but it's always there."

The genderflux flag consists of five horizontal stripes, with each color representing a different aspect of the identity: the light blue symbolizes masculinity, the light pink represents femininity, the grey signifies neutrality or the absence of gender, the dark pink indicates a stronger connection to femininity, and the dark blue reflects a stronger connection to masculinity. This color scheme captures the dynamic and fluctuating nature of genderflux.

Colors and fabric used:

Couleur : rose
Dimension : 206 x 97,6 cm
Textile : tulle

Couleur : rose clair
Dimension : 206 x 97,6 cm
Textile : coton

Couleur : gris
Dimension : 111 x 97,6 cm
Textile : synthétique (style imperméable)

Couleur : bleu clair
Dimension : 197 x 99,7 cm
Textile : synthétique

Couleur : bleu
Dimension : 111 x 99,2 cm
Textile : coton

Couleur : jaune
Dimension : 192 x 99,2 cm
Textile : tulle

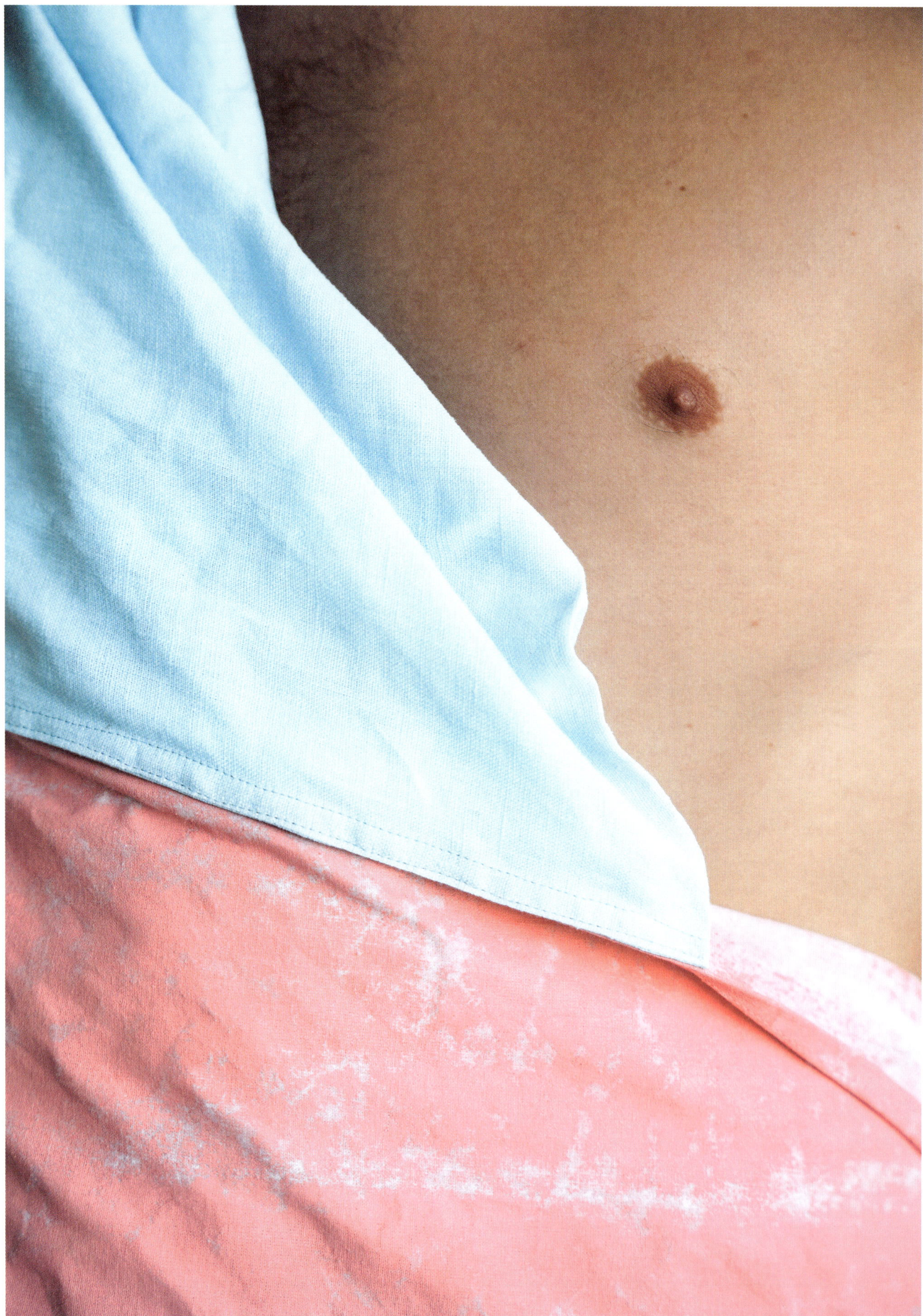

Genderfaun

Colors and fabric used:

Couleur : Orange
Dimension : 206 x 97,6 cm
Textile : Synthétique (style
          peluche)

Couleur : Jaune foncé
Dimension : 192 x 99,2 cm
Textile : Coton léger (un
peu transparent)

Couleur : Jaune clair
Dimension : 206 x 97,6 cm
Textile : Synthétique
          transparent

Couleur : Bleu
Dimension : 192 x 99,2 cm
Textile : Synthétique
          (effet cuir)

Couleur : Gris
Dimension : 111 x 97,6 cm
Textile : Synthétique
          (style imperméable)

Couleur : Mauve
Dimension : 111 x 97,6 cm
Textile : Coton

Genderfaun, also known as Genderfawn, is a form of genderfluidity that excludes women-aligned or fiaspec genders. Individuals who identify as genderfaun typically do not experience feminine genders unless those genders are also aligned with masculinity, such as the term "rosboy." Genderfaun falls under the broader genderfaunet umbrella, which encompasses various non-binary identities.

The genderfaun flag features colors that reflect this identity, though the specific colors can vary. Generally, the flag is designed to represent the nuances of genderfaun experience, emphasizing a connection to masculine identities while recognizing the fluid nature of gender. The combination of colors symbolizes the diversity within genderfaun identities and their distinction from more traditionally feminine experiences.

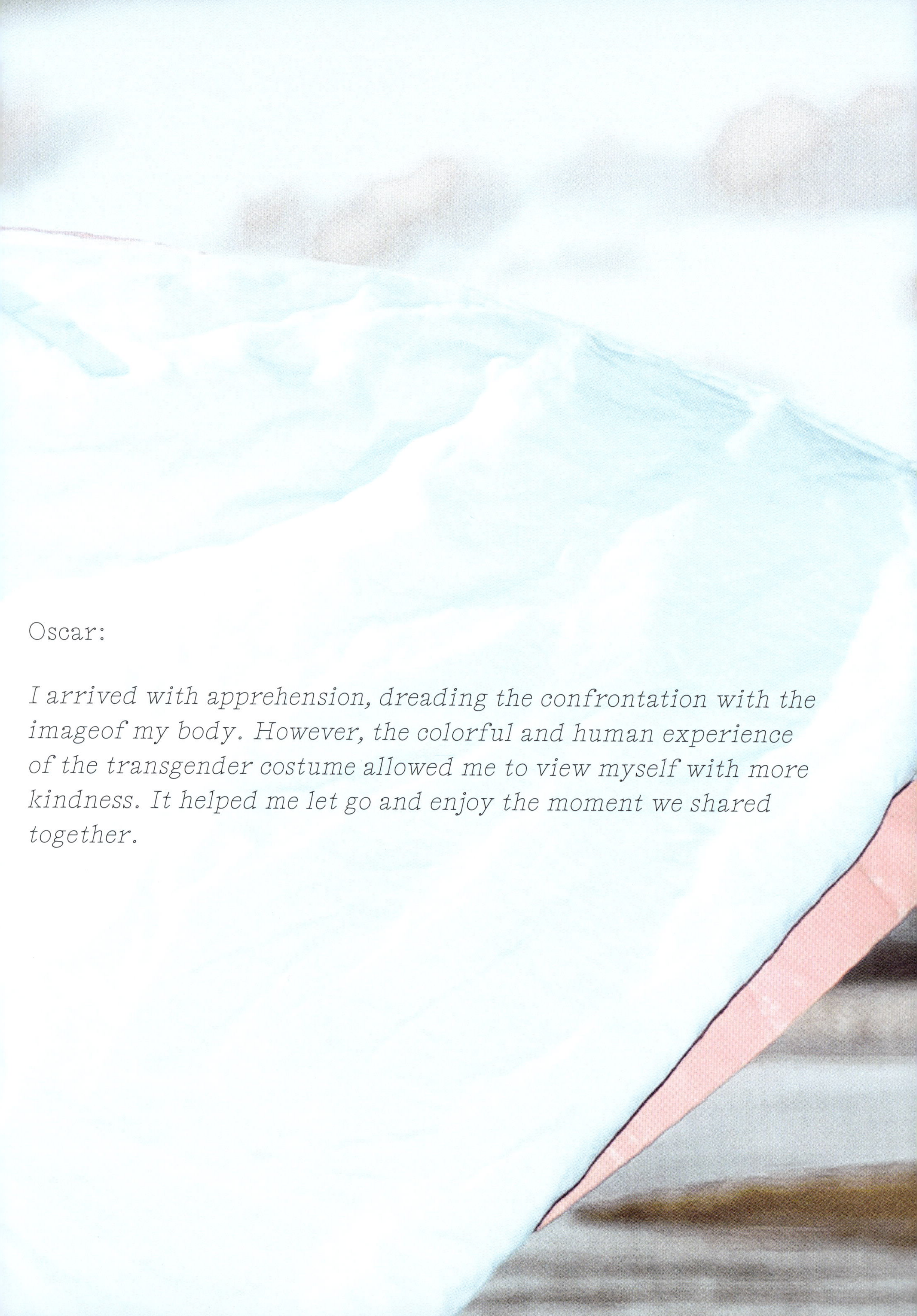

Oscar:

I arrived with apprehension, dreading the confrontation with the imageof my body. However, the colorful and human experience of the transgender costume allowed me to view myself with more kindness. It helped me let go and enjoy the moment we shared together.

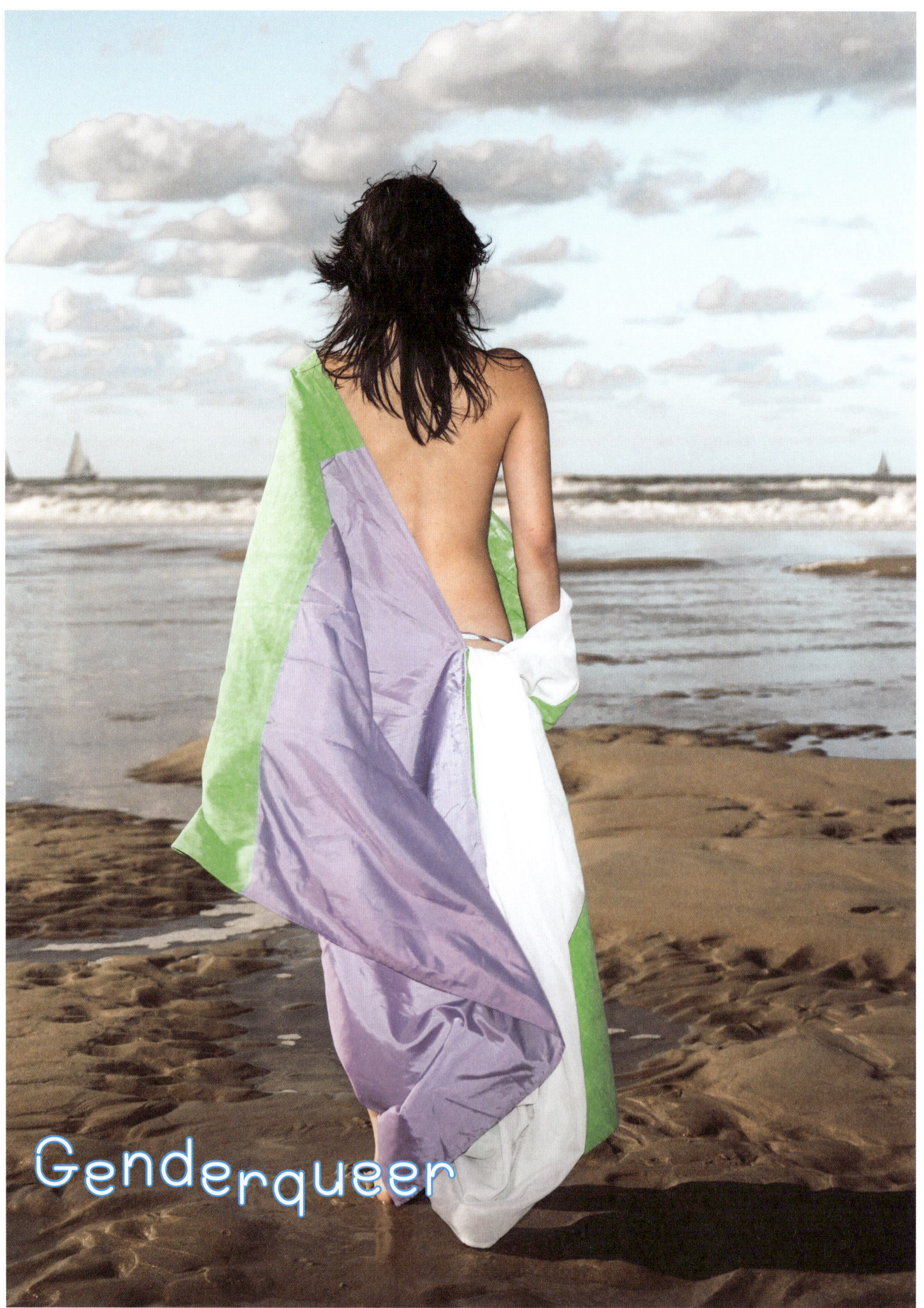
Genderqueer

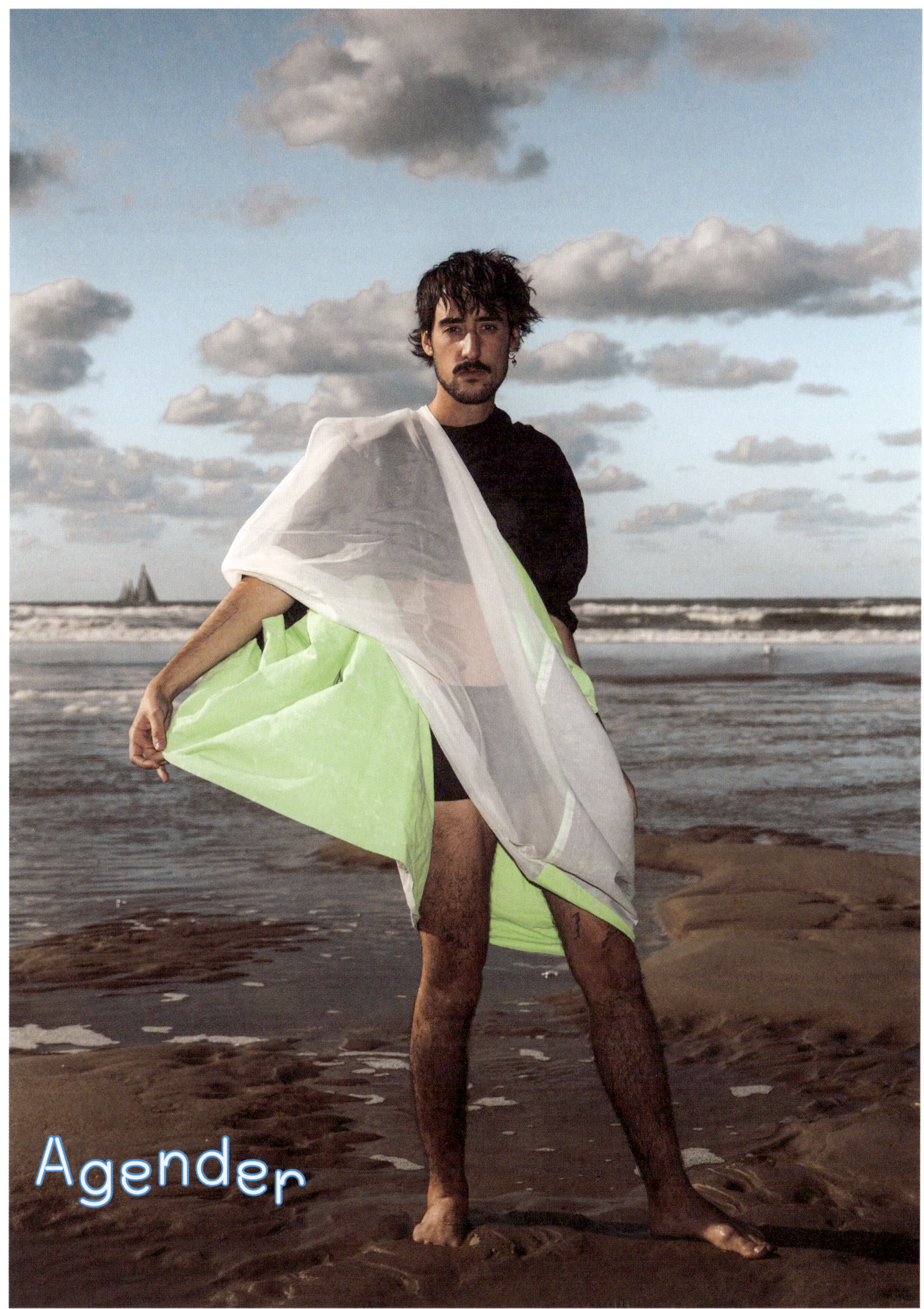
Agender

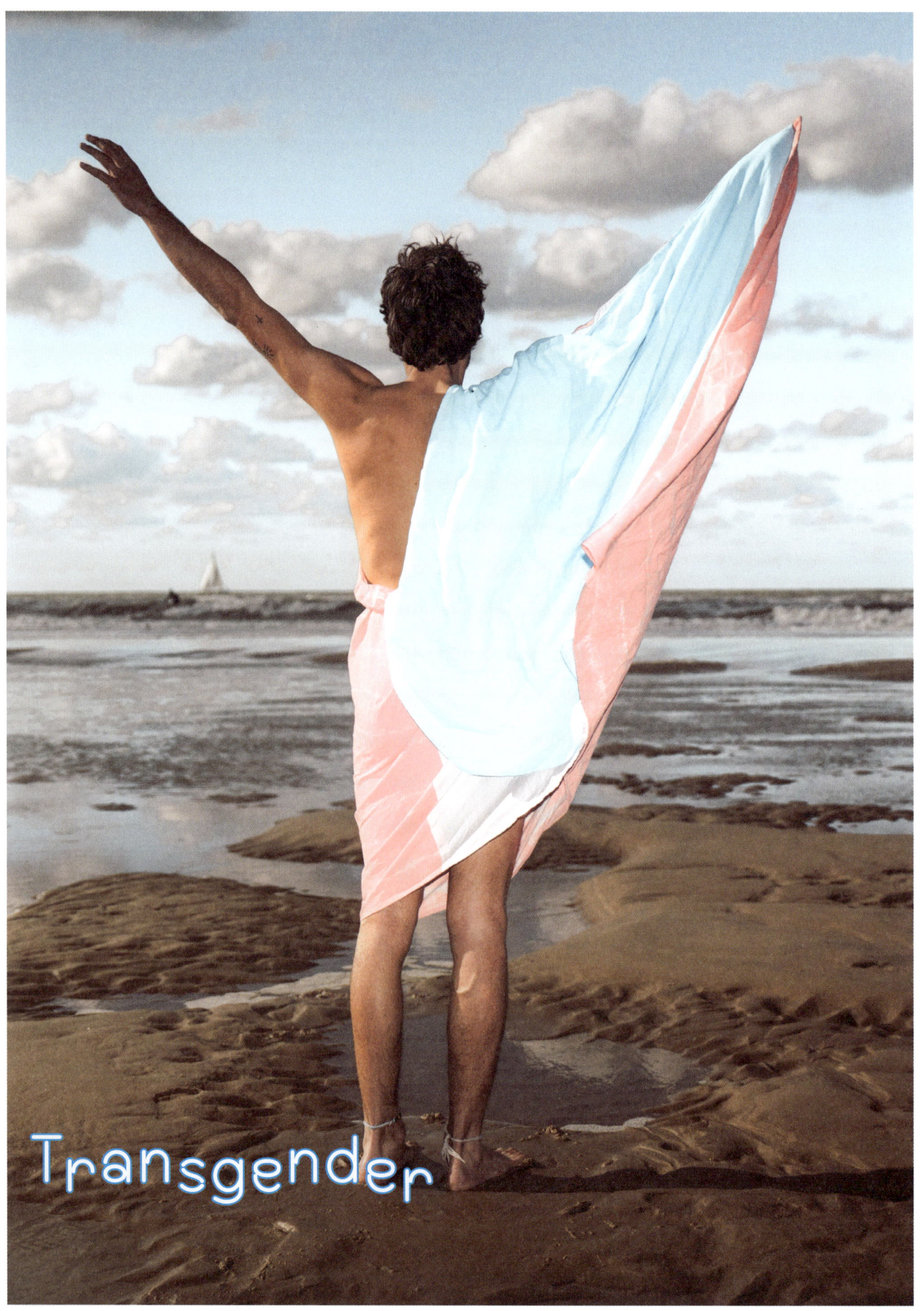
Transgender

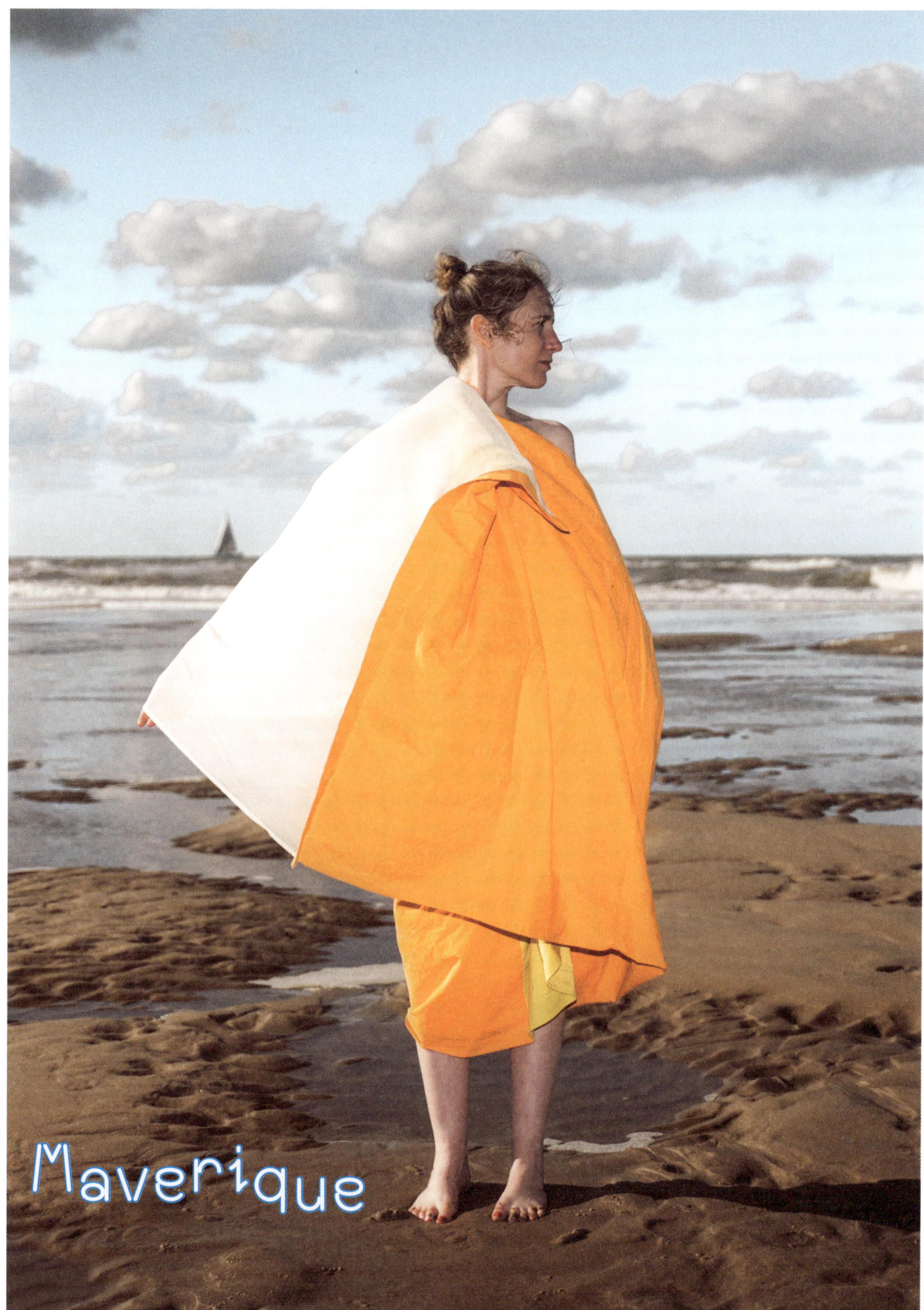
Maverique

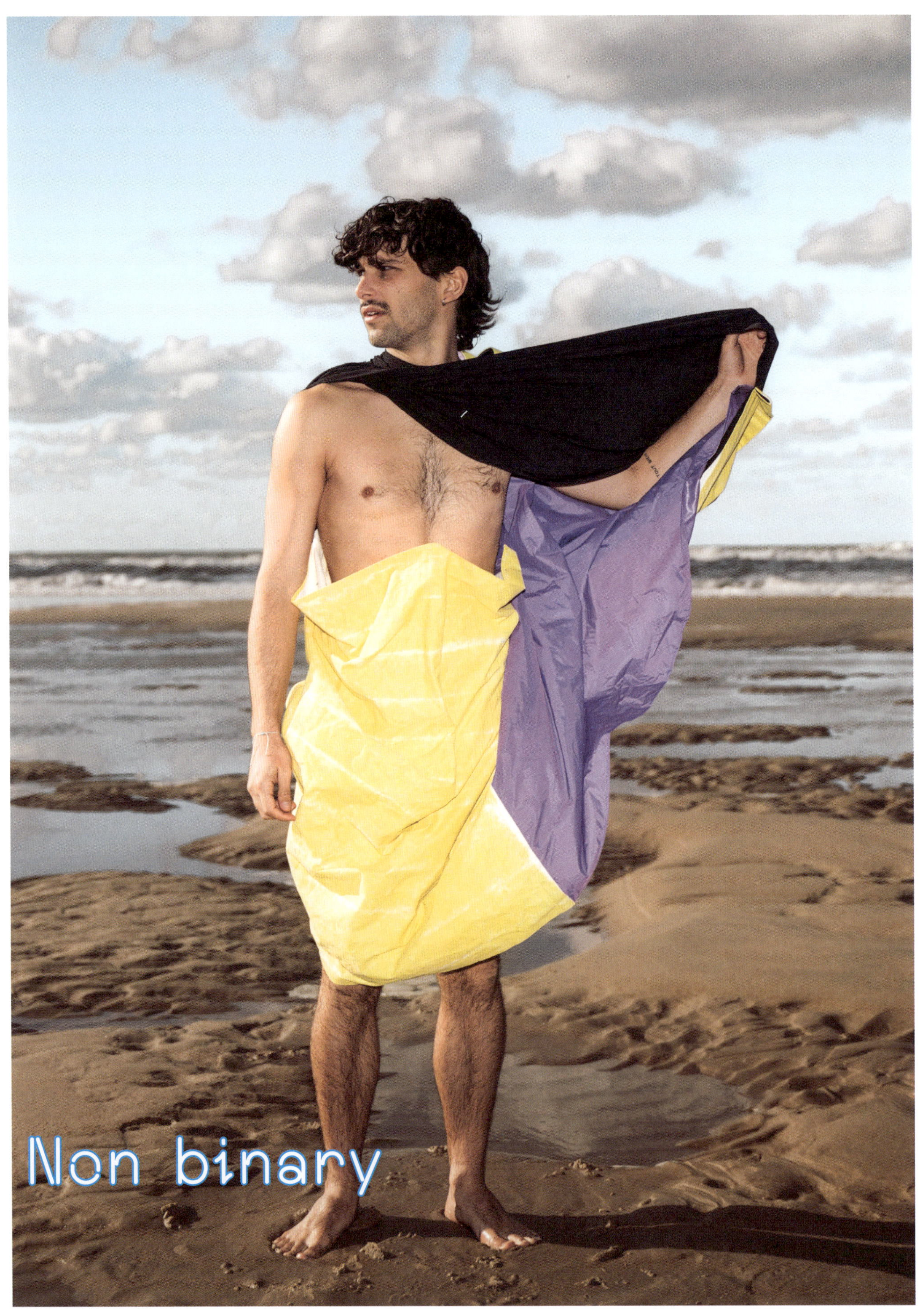
Non binary

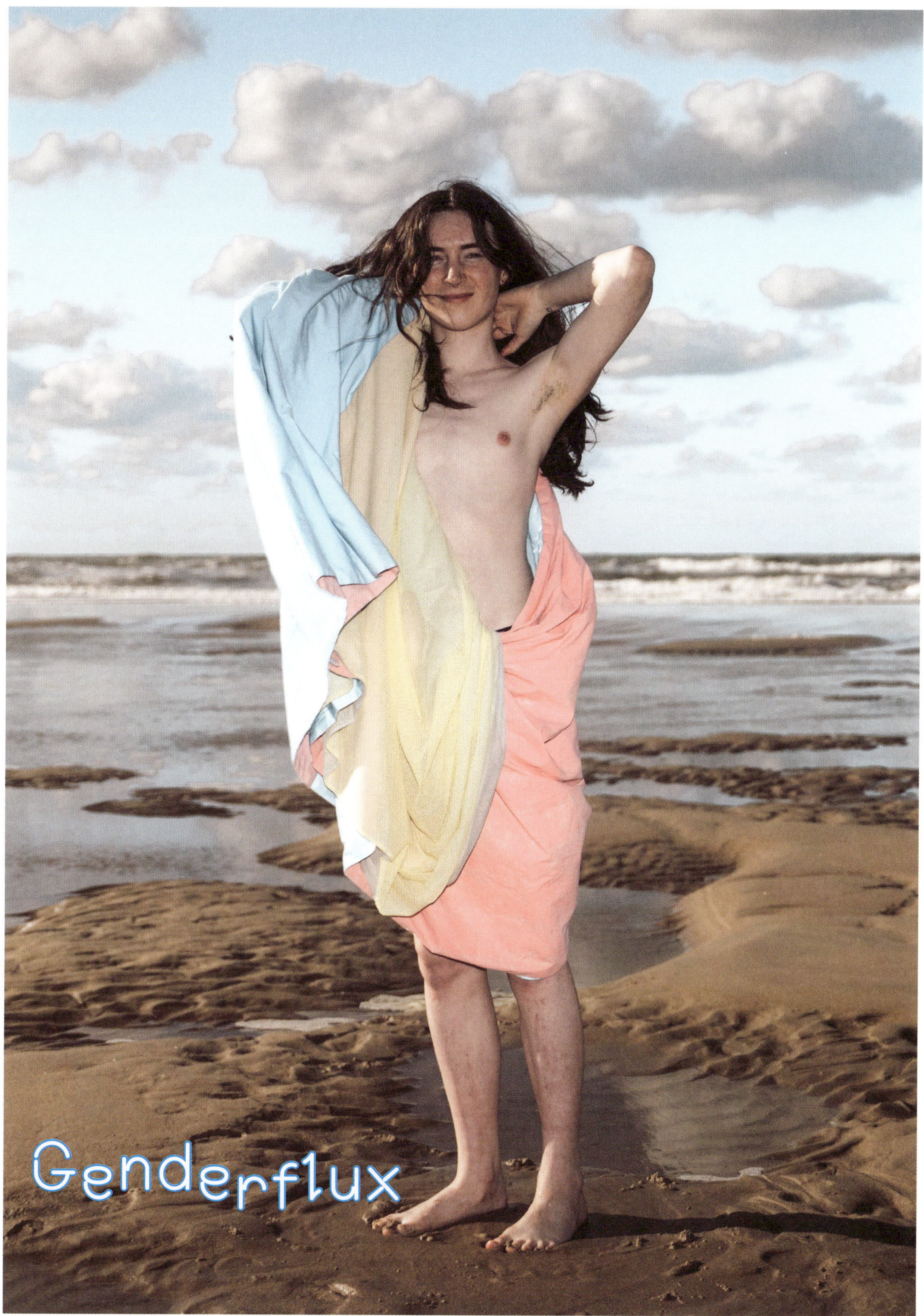

Genderflux

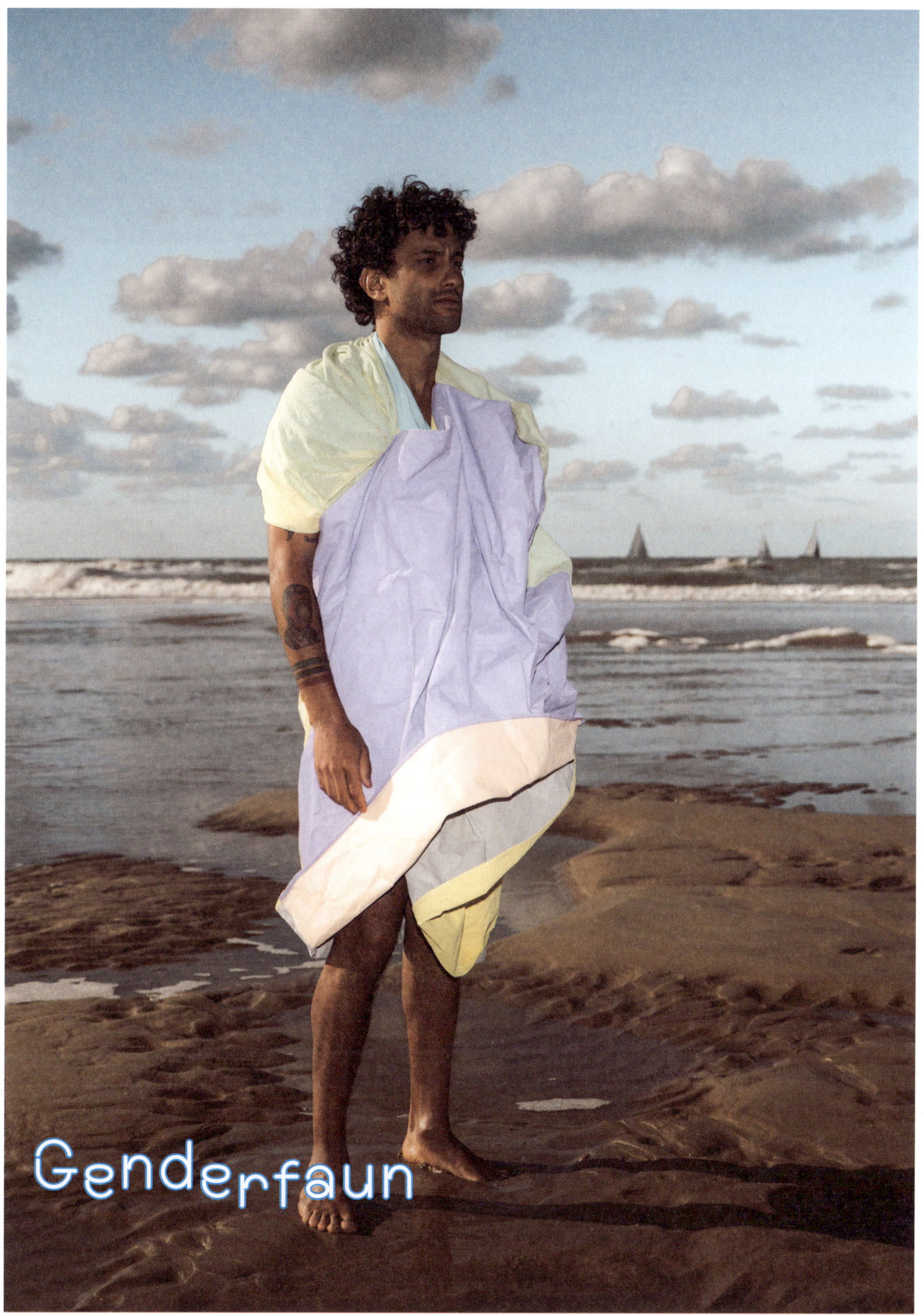
Genderfaun

| Description of the work: | The happening of the parade, *What's going on?* is an animated situation, sudden dynamic confusion, and/or agitation between people in a public space. The parade is composed out of people that carry (wear) from 8 till 12 costumes, banners, or objects. These are inhabited paintings, pieces of clothing designed to be worn in a type of ritual dance with the intention to denounce. They are first activated by performers and can then, gradually be taken over by members of the public who can join the happening. |

| External factors influencing the work: | Important is to have dry weather, and to have a wall or border in a material that catches the sound of the live music. |

| Requirements for Documentation: | None |

| Artwork requirements: | The parade is composed out of 8 to 12 people that carry (wear) costumes, banners or objects. These are inhabited paintings, pieces of clothing designed to be worn in a type of ritual dance with the intention to denounce. They are activated by 12 chosen performers (including the artist and an assistant). The costumes can then gradually be taken over by members of the public who can join the happening. These can be passed again to other people |

the performance script

Anyone may use this script
to live the performance,
free to deviate from it.

Artist: LDB+

Title: Parade, what's going on?

Year: 2023

Medium: happening including dance,
               movement with several objects,
               costumes, banners, and music

Dimensions: variable

walking the circle. After 20 seconds, a first performer leaves the circle, goes to the inner field inscribed in the circle, and starts activating the costume, dancing, running, moving and expressing a personal discovery of the form, textures and colors of the costume. 10 to 30 seconds later a second performer joins the inner circle. This process goes on until all performers are now activating their costume. At this moment, the artist starts to designate the performers one by one to go to the public and invite the audience to take over their costume and join the parade. This process goes on for around 30 minutes.

PERFORMERS:

Total number: 8 to 12 of mixed gender and queer identities, aged 18 years or above.
The artist, the artist-assistant and 6 to 10 chosen performers start with the activation.

All the performers are exchanging their costumes during the activation with participants out of the public. These participants are introduced in the concept of the activation and guided by the artist, assistant or one of the 10 original performers to handle the exchange of the costume.

All the performers and members of the public that join the activation must be in general good health and with a body constitution that allows wearing the costume and are at least 18 years old.

of the audience who want to participate and activate the work.

The parade is supposed to allow a moment of shared joy and installs a collective feeling of being different, being other. This difference is adored and no longer hidden in this moment and place installed by this happening. The participants can behave and act in the way they want to. For the viewers it should make a clear political statement of acceptance and the beauty of otherness.

The parade starts in a circle, face to the outside and holding hands with each other. This moment takes like 3 minutes and is a form of concentration to enter the performance. Then, on the sign of the artist, every participant declares all together the following text of Lygia Clark loud and clearly:

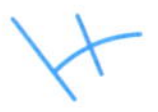

"We (the artists) are the proposers: we are the mold: it is up to you to breathe the meaning of our existence into it. We are the proposers: our proposition is that of a dialogue. Alone we do not exist. We are at your mercy. We are the proposers: we have buried the work of art as such, and we call upon you so that thought may survive through your action. We are the proposers: we do not propose you with either the past, or the future, but the now."

After this declaration the music starts, and the 12 performers start

take over the costume and join the
happening. This process goes on as
long as there are candidates. The
invited members of the audience
should have a body constitution that
allows wearing the costume, should
be at least 18 years old and should be
in good general health.

Logistics:

The artist and assistant are present
for each activation. The costs for
presenting the work are the insur-
ance costs of the costumes (average
each costume costs 2500 euro) and
the fee, travel and accommodation
costs for the musician(s), the artist,
the assistant and the 10 original performers.
   Before and after the activation,
the different costumes and
objects are hanged on 12 coat
hangers on a coatrack of approx. 2
m long and 2 m heigh on wheels that
can be stored or on display before or
after the activation. These hangers
and the coatrack must be provided
by the hosting institution.
A changing room for the artist,
assistant and the 10 original
performers should be available to
dress up for the parade.

The 10 original performers are
previously instructed and have
practiced together with the
artist and the assistant this
activation. They are volunteers
and agree to do the activation for
personal exploration of their
(sexual) otherness. They agree
that pictures or video can be
taken by external persons out of
the audience or the press.
　　　These performers are
locally found in communities of
queer or gender support groups.
The collaboration is guided during a time of preparation that is
defined beforehand in mutual
consultation.
　　　The music is provided by
(a) local musician(s), approved by
the artist. The musician(s) are
available during the repetitions
of the activation as well as during
the actual public performance.

A spontaneous participation is
required as the work must be
activated by the audience.
To provoke that participation,
different strategies are elaborat-
ed. The 8 to12 original performers
that start the parade have been
introduced in the conceptual
framework of the parade and are
called during the performance by
the artist to go, one by one, to a
member of the public they think
would be interesting to participate. They talk to them explain-
ing the project and invite them to

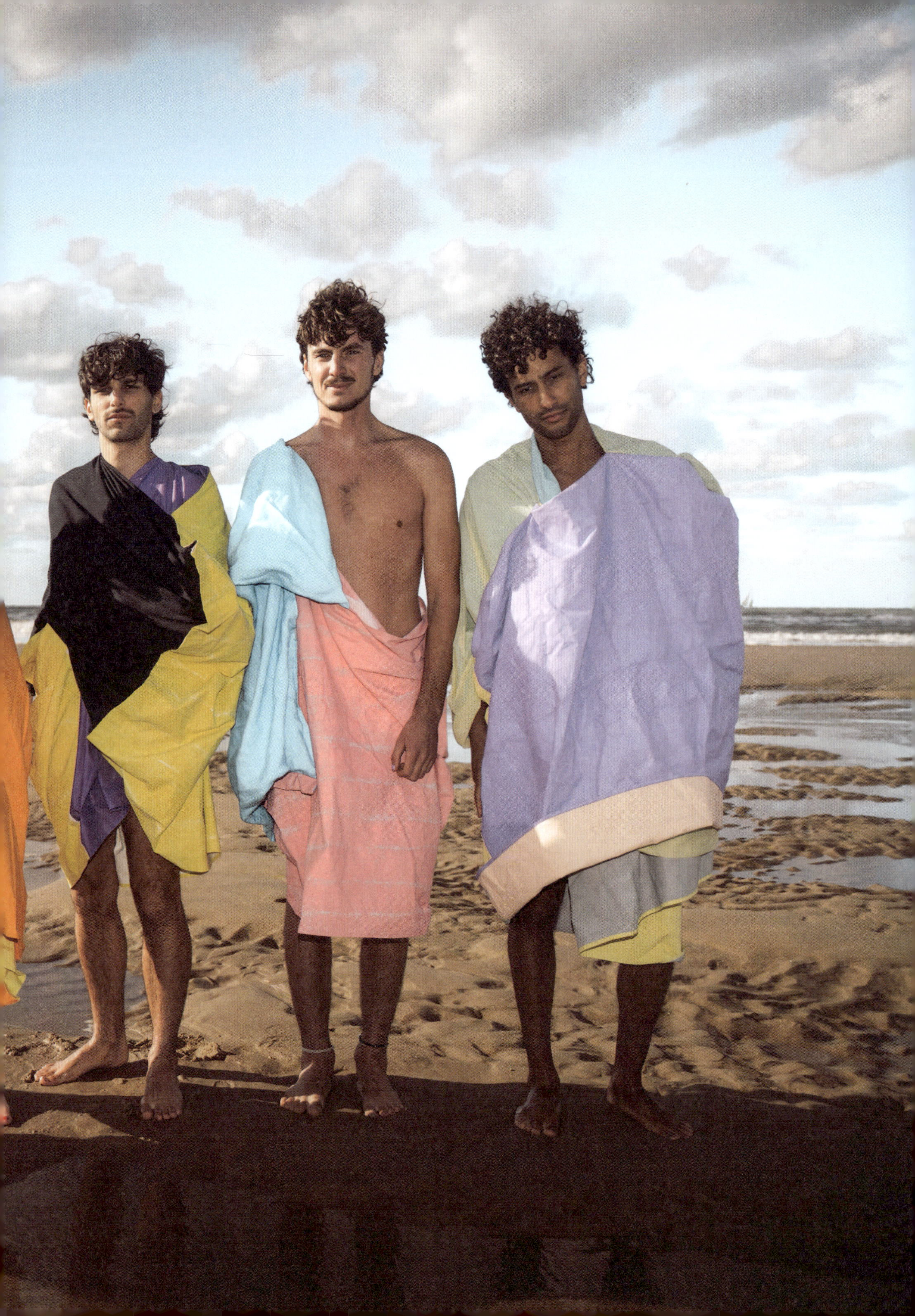

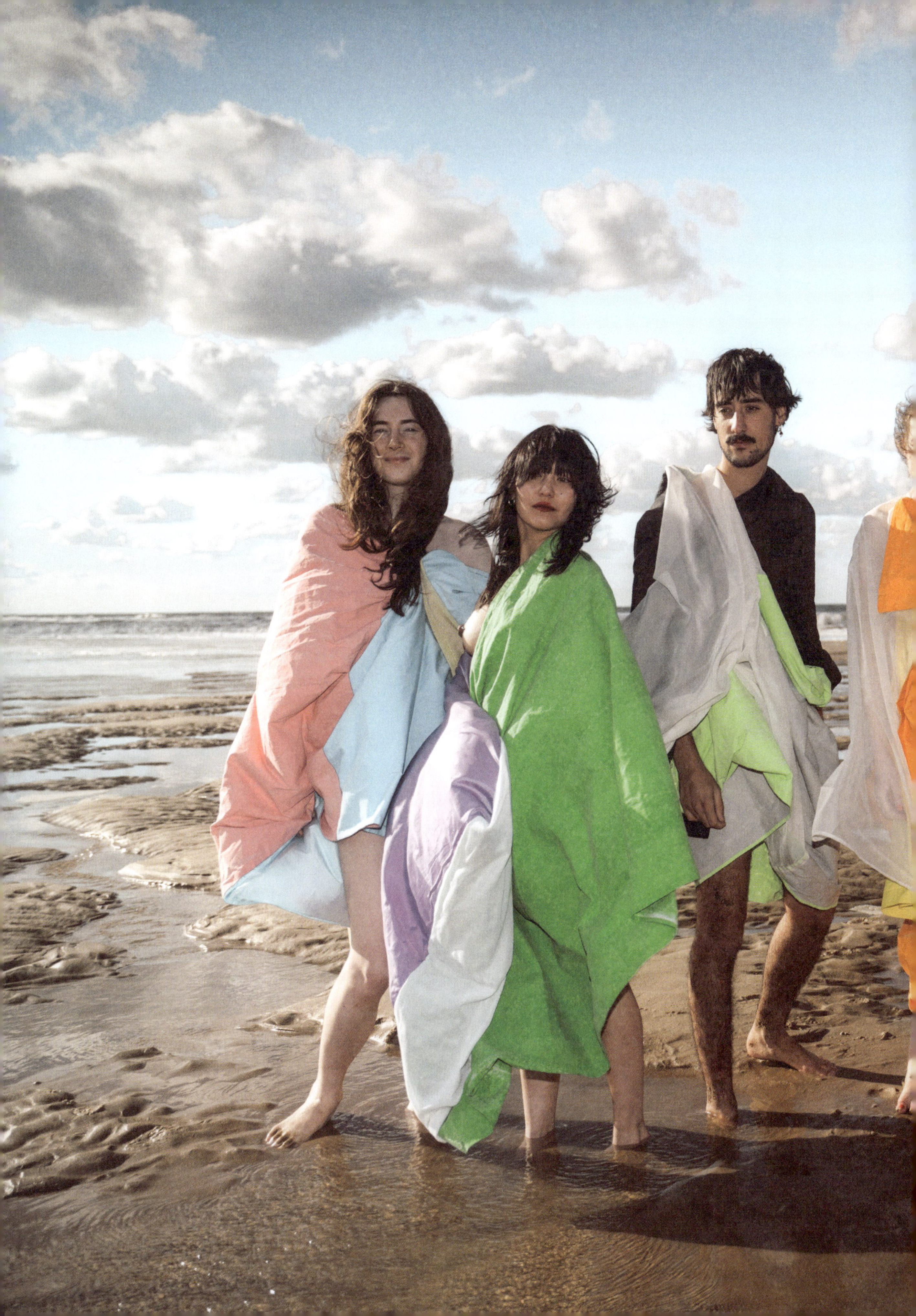

The politics of *Parangolés*, writes art historian Irene Small, are "transitive and transferrable". [4] Their movement is ambulatory and unpredictable – one just needs to look at the mesmerising figure of Nininha of Xoxoba, star of the Mangueira samba school and the Rio Carnaval in the 1960s, as she twirls in *Parangolé Capa 21*, which Oiticica dedicated to her. [5] Whereas some *Parangolés* invite more jagged and geometric movements, Xoxoba's *Parangolé* – the same reprised by De Boeck in Kassel – seems to incite trance-like torsions.

In their volatility, evanescence and shape shifting, the *Parangolés* make light of art's traditional benchmarks of recognisability, formal coherence and durability. They envelop the wearers/users, as well as the bystanders/co-participants, into a zone of corporeal and affective discovery. As Oiticica put it, the *Parangolés* represent an "ambient proposal" [6], an immersive throbbing, almost indistinguishable from 'daily life', in which to lose oneself, and one's subjectivity, and fall into a vaster, less charted space. In his irruption at documenta and subsequent rhythmic appearances, De Boeck harnesses the power of the *Parangolés* to offer glimmers of a different social dynamic, one based on collective, participatory, anonymised and aleatory alliances. This dynamic is *queer*, insofar as it destabilises the binary logics that regulate gendered and sexual roles and performances, bringing bodies and textile objects into sensorial flux. It is, moreover, *cruisy* because it activates and deregulates the spaces around and between such encounters: every interstice, every gap opens onto uncharted zones of communicative sensibility.

[4] Irene V. Small, *Hélio Oiticica: Folding the Frame* (Chicago, London: The University of Chicago Press, 2016), 220.

[5] See Ivan Cardoso, *H.O.*, 35 mm film, 13 minutes, 1979: https://vimeo.com/100591883 (accessed 8 August 2024).

[6] Fernando Bruno, Between Carnaval and Mondrian: The Manifold Influences on Brazilian artist Hélio Oiticica , post: notes on art in a global context, 8 November 2017: https://post.moma.org/between-carnaval-and-mondrian-the-manifold-influences-on-brazilian-artist-helio-oiticica/ (accessed 9 September 2024)

Twist and Turns
in Lieven De Boeck's recent work.

written by Antony Hudek

Without invitation or permission, the artist Lieven De Boeck staged the hour-long performance *The World as Museum* in several locations near the official sites of the documenta fifteen exhibition in Kassel in 2022. The unauthorised interventions saw two participants twist and turn, gyrate and wrestle in and with loosely fitting outfits resembling flags, capes or ponchos, to the live improvisation of a saxophone.[1] *The World as Museum* belongs to a series of performative actions in a larger research project by De Boeck entitled *The Archive of Disappearance*, in which participants interact in art-related public spaces wearing textile forms modelled on *Parangolés* by the Brazilian artist Hélio Oiticica (1937–1980).

Oiticica's *Parangolés* are neither costumes nor accessories for performative actions. They are *embodiments* of life practices which twist the lines that determine our affective and physical behaviours. In the 1960s slang of Brazilian favelas, *Parangolé* translates as "What's going on?"[2] For Oiticica, the *Parangolés'* interrogative open-endedness allowed "for a lived creative experience" that would "give to today's individual the possibility of 'experiencing creation', of discovering through participation, on many levels, something that for him has meaning."[3]

[1] Lieven De Boeck, *The World as Museum: Re-enactment Parangolé Capa 22, Xoxoba of Hélio Oiticica*, documenta fifteen, 14 September 2022, 4–5 pm, with Thomas Gibault (dancer), Christina Fuchs (music), Emma Revest (dancer) and the audience.

[2] Marc Pottier, introduction to Delmari Romero Keith, *Hélio Oiticica: Parangolé* (Milan: Mousse Publishing, 2023): https://www.moussemagazine.it/publishing/helio-oitici-ca-book-2022/ (accessed 6 August 2024).

[3] Hélio Oiticica, Posição e Programma , Aspiro ao Grande Labirinto, ed. by Luciano Figueiredo, Lygia Pape and Waly Salomão (Rio de Janeiro: Rocco, 1986), 111, quoted in Celso Favaretto, Tropicália: The Explosion of the Obvious , in Tropicália: a Revolution in Brazilian Culture (1967 1972), edited by Carlos Basualdo (São Paulo: Cosac Naify, 2005), 89.

stored. For De Boeck, the fire provided a paradoxical double opportunity: to borrow from Oiticica without falling into the opposition of original vs copy and, at the same time, to give new life to the fundamental insights of Oiticica's experimentation with the transience and collective agency of textiles and bodies. It is indirectly thanks to the fire that De Boeck landed on *Oiticica's Parangolé P25 Capa 21 "Xoxoba"* (1968) as a model for his own. The only surviving version of P25 was an exhibition copy preserved at Kunstinstituut Melly (then Witte de With), which organised Oiticia's first retrospective in 1992 and where De Boeck had his first major solo exhibition in 2004. With the institution as deferred meeting ground and facilitator, De Boeck could study the original copy up close, in its finest detail.

Oiticica introduced his *Parangolés* at the opening of a group exhibition in the gardens of the Museum of Modern Art in Rio de Janeiro in 1965, after museum officials refused to allow the samba dancers clad in the artist's outfits to enter the building. Echoing this episode, a year after his first appearance at documenta, De Boeck expanded his reactivation of Oiticica's *Parangolés* – this time under the title *What's Going On?*, and with prior permission – outside of the Sarasota Art Museum in Florida, with musicians and students of the nearby Ringling College of Art and Design. The students created their own *Parangolé*-inspired outfits reflecting their individual queer identities. In the passage from Rio in 1965 to Sarasota in 2023, De Boeck emphasises the queer underpinnings of Oiticica's institutional interruptions. As Bradley Webster observes, the choice of organising *What's Going On?* in the viciously anti-LGBTQIA+ context of contemporary Florida is particularly bold, as is the choice of confronting the state's discrimination not with violence or protest but with an openly queer, jubilatory procession.[9]

Through De Boeck's recursive retellings of Oiticica's *Parangolés*, one arrives at a more intimate sensation of what animates certain queer movements in art. In

[9] Bradley Webster, 'When Is Art' in the Queer State of Florida?', Noah Becker's Whitehot Magazine of Contemporary Art, 8 January 2024: https://whitehotmagazine.com/articles/in-queer-state-florida-/6165 (accessed 9 August 2024).

Twisting theirstories

In his novel *Nicolas Pages*, queer author Guillaume Dustan praises the combination of dancing under the influence (in his case, of ecstasy), producing sensations that find expression in twirling, "after which my head starts to turn, it's perfect. I've rediscovered the secret of dervishes, my sweethearts. Small children know this too: spinning like a top is euphoric. The movement of life is like an endless screw turning upon itself and, in so doing, drilling."[7] Screwing, spewing, excreting – such were the terms Oiticica used in the early 1970s to encourage the evacuation of the conformist, patriarchal provincialism he saw taking over Brazil's avantgarde under the name (which he himself had supported several years prior, but now disavowed) of *Tropicália.*[8]

De Boeck's *Parangolés* take a different tack than Oiticica's visceral rejection of reactionary tendencies, acknowledging the fifty-year distance that separates them. From one queer artist to another, far from historical mimicry, De Boeck's bond to Oiticica – and to queer artistic genealogy in general – is reparative, even caring. In this, De Boeck's relation to his forebearer is emblematic of a generation of queer artists old enough to have seen the ravages of the AIDS pandemic up close, yet young enough to have escaped the fate met by many practitioners born in the 1960s and before. Old enough, that is, to have experienced the widespread unquestioned invisibilisation and criminalisation of homosexuality, yet young enough to overlap with the growing recognition – and more recently, recuperation – of queer cultures.

De Boeck's attentiveness towards Oiticica as transhistorical co-participant is all the more respectful, and significant, since almost nothing remains of the Brazilian artist's original textile works. Their traces were nearly completely eradicated in 2009 when a fire engulfed the warehouse where much of the artist's estate was

[7] Guillaume Dustan, *Nicolas Pages* (1999), in *Œuvres II* (Paris: P.O.L., 2021), 208. (Author's translation).

[8] See Hélio Oiticica, "Brasil diarréia" (1970), in *Arte brasileira hoje* (Rio de Janeiro: Paz e terra, 1973): https://icaa.mfah.org/s/en/item/1090409 (accessed 29 September 2024).

This lack of spatial definition is both the result and the cause of the *Parangolé* as a research process. It is unsettled, not so much context-less as always on the look-out for a context that, because of its dependency on the wearer/user, will inevitably shift. Wherever it appears, the *Parangolé* activates a "social de-conditioning"[14] that defies the logic of efficiency and competitive economy, its oscillations and spin threatening at any moment to veer out of control.

Queer textility

Although the warehouse fire sealed their disappearance and subsequent re-emergence in De Boeck's work, Oiticica's *Parangolés* were all but destined to disappear. Textiles, for one, are supremely unstable, vulnerable to the "impurities" of biological life – humidity, oxidation, light, dust.[15] To make matters worse, the *Parangolés* stood little chance to survive as archival documents given their actively encouraged (mis)usage. In the wake of the fire, Irene Small remarks on both the shortsightedness of celebrating the destruction "to utterly dematerialise Oiticica's production" and its fetishisation by museums as relics. Between these two extremes, Small suggests that reconstructions of Oiticica's work "will be three-dimensional diagrams: non-sites, to use Robert Smithson's term, that necessarily refer us away from the objects themselves. … [S]uch diagrams will be both literal and performative, thematizing their distance from the objects, spaces, and experiences they represent."[16]

While compelling, Small's diagrammatic resolution of the either/or tension posed by Oiticica's art after the fire runs the risk of missing the unalienable physicality of the artist's work – that is to say, its queer textures. The tactility and malleability of

[12] Eve Kosofsky Sedgwick, "Queer Performativity: Henry James *The Art of the Novel*", *GLQ: A Journal of Lesbian and Gay Studies*, Vol. 1, 1993, p. 2.

[13] *Oiticica in London*, edited by Guy Brett and Luciano Figueiredo (London: Tate Publishing, 2007), 112.

[14] Carlos Basualdo, "Tropicália: Avant-Garde, Popular Culture, and the Culture Industry in Brazil", in *Tropicália: a Revolution*, 17.

[15] "Purity is a myth" is the title of Oiticica's installation *Penetrable PN2* (1966–67).

[16] Irene V. Small, "Hélio Oiticica", *Artforum* (February 2010): https://www.artforum.com/columns/helio-oiticica-193450/ (accessed 3 August 2024).

De Boeck's *The Archive of Disappearance*, it is not simply a matter of showing the *Parangolés* – of making a radical past visible again, for posterity. Rather, De Boeck twists and turns the textile "work actions" and "trans-objects" (Oiticica's terms), thereby recasting their originating impulse each time anew according to changing circumstances. De Boeck himself describes his relation to historical references in terms of a "queer temporality", akin to cruising, which causes "a temporal disruption that intertwines past, present, and future, contrasting sharply with the linear time focus of classic academic research." [10] De Boeck, one could say, cruises queer histories, connecting with Oiticica in an imagined, loving *pas de deux* (or *de trois*, or *quatre*…).This temporal fluidity allows the artwork to exist "in a state of perpetual becoming, constantly redefined by the desires and inter-actions of those who engage with it." [11] Continually repositioned in the flow of the present, De Boeck's re-embodiments of Oiticica's *Parangolés* are subject to unexpected adaptations and slippages. They form part of a contingent, immaterial archive teetering on the verge of disappearance, falling in and out of visibility, ever ready to be revived differently.

Theorist Eve Kosofsky Sedwick has written of the referentiality of performativity in queer contexts as "mutually perverse" and "aberrant". [12] Queer temporality affects not only the aberrant referentiality and mutual perversion between De Boeck's and Oiticica's *Parangolés,* but also of De Boeck's own *Parangolés.* Inter-woven between them is a belief in the queering power of art to upset existing distributions of power and to explore the morphing boundaries of identity. To trace these non-linear relationships between temporalities and places, De Boeck adopts an unresolved searching motion that was, for Oiticica, a defining charac-teristic of the *Parangolé*:

> *The cape is not an object but a searching process, searching for the roots of the objective birth of the work, the direct perceptive moulding of it. This is why its constructive method is popular and primitive, refer-ring to flags, tents, capes, etc. It is not a finished object and its spatial sense is not definite.* [13]

[10] Lieven De Boeck, Letter to the Art World: Let s Go Queer!
[11] Lieven De Boeck, Letter to the Art World".

Five days after De Boeck organised *What's Going On?* on the grounds of the Sarasota Art Museum, the students and musicians performed again at the opening of the 2023 Untitled Art fair in Miami Beach, as part of its official programme of events responding to the annual theme "Gender Equality in the Arts".[20] While the procession at the art museum echoed the origins of Oiticica's *Parangolés*, its re-appearance within an art fair conveyed a starkly different, more sombre meaning. What stands out in the video recordings of De Boeck's Untitled Art performance is the slowness of the procession and the music, a far cry from Oiticica's samba rhythms, not to speak of the frenetic pace of the fair. During the half-hour performance, the students speak aloud well-known lines by Lygia Clark from 1968, "We are the proposers, we are the mould, it is up to you to breathe the meaning of our existence into it…" By slowing down the *Parangolés'* twirls with art students at an art fair, and associating Oiticica with Clark, De Boeck addresses head-on the art market's commodification of queer enthusiasm, participation and collaboration. Performing in close succession at a Florida art museum and an art fair allowed *What's Going On?* to show the two sites to be, despite their apparent differences, deeply linked: the right-wing backlash against personal expression in the public realm goes hand-in-hand with the marketing of queerness as emblems of inclusion and diversity.

The *Parangolé* enables De Boeck to play with these contradictions, to wrap his practice in them to eschew the possibility of resolution and generate yet uncharted identity formations and forms of belonging. The *Parangolé* acts as a rite of passage; it makes passages possible in, through and besides the fixed alternatives laid out within heterosexist normativity for, but also by, queer cultures. For Oiticica, the *Parangolé* was an outcome of "passing through the object" to attain "experience", where the activator's body constituted the main site of interpersonal agency. De Boeck's own passage through the *Parangolé* results in a different, more diffuse movement, where the disruptive power of

[19] André Lepecki, "Affective Geometry, Immanent Acts: Lygia Clark and Performance", Part 1, *post: notes on art in a global context*, 8 August 2017: https://post.moma.org/part-1-affective-geometry-immanent-acts-lygia-clark-and-performance/ (accessed 5 August 2024).

[20] Kame Hame, "Diversity and Inclusion Art are at the Heart of Untitled Art Miami Beach 2023", *Widewalls*, 8 November 2023: https://www.widewalls.ch/magazine/untitled-art-2023 (accessed 9 August 2023).

textile, its resistance to organisation and structure through mangling and twisting, is a powerful, and queer, connection between Oiticica and De Boeck. About the sense of touch, Kosofsky Sedgwick notes that:

> *it makes nonsense out of any dualistic understanding of agency and passivity; to touch is always already to reach out, to fondle, to heft, to tap, or to enfold, and always also to understand other people or natural forces as having effectually done so before oneself, if only in the making of the textured object.* [17]

Textile can thus only ever be plural, collective, denying the wearer/user the illusion of being alone in experiencing their complex sensorial phenomenology. The collective sensuality of textile is especially important in Oiticica's artistic development as well as in that of his friend, the artist Lygia Clark. Both went from 'neo-concrete' objects in the late 1950s and early 1960s – still beholden to structure and frame – to more intimate and transient objects capable of withstanding, indeed of encouraging folding, cutting, twisting and crumpling. Through textile, Clark and Oiticica de-structured and surrendered tradition-al artistic materials (canvas, stone and metal) to organic life, transforming their surface illusion of coherence into the unmappable topographies of individual and social bodies. Once unstretched and distorted, twisted and turned, textile reveals a (dis)organisation that hovers, writes Kosofsky Sedgwick, "just below the level of shape or structure." [18] Through touching, tearing, creasing and folding, textile's quasi-structure reveals – not so much diagrammatically as physically –the fragility and unexpectedness of social and sensual contact. In terms that resonate with Oiticica's *Parangolés*, André Lepecki writes that Clark's "assimilation of objects with bodies, this incorporation of the environment in a deeply sensuous process … could only occur through an engaged practice 'simultaneously personal and collective', where one's 'own eroticism' was assured by a 'community experience' in the creation of propositions." [19]

[17] Eve Kosofsky Sedgwick, *Touching Feeling: Affect, Pedagogy, Performativity* (Durham, London: Duke University Press, 2003), 14–15.

[18] Kosofsky Sedgwick, *Touching, feeling*, 16.

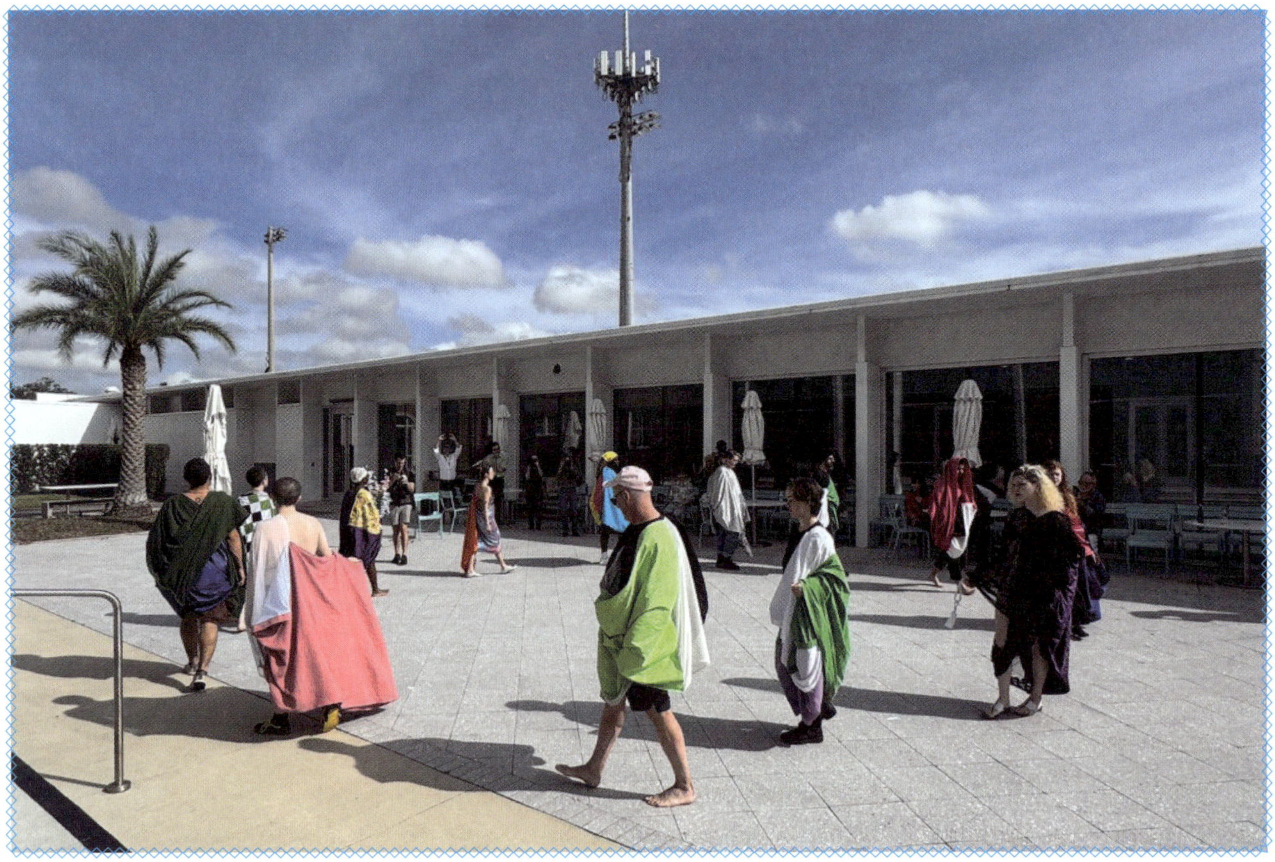

Performance Public Square Sarasota Art Museum

Performance Public Square Sarasota Art Museum

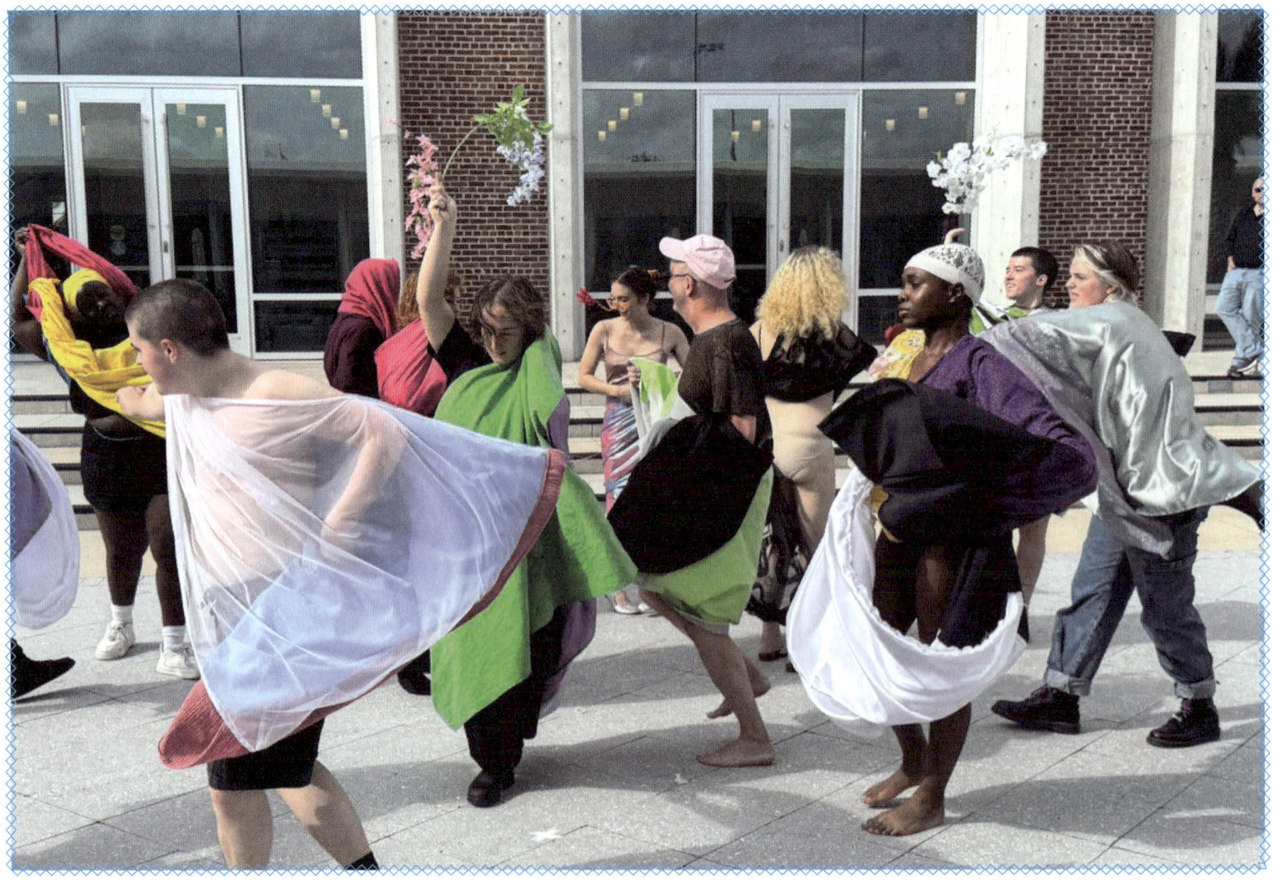

Oiticica's trans-objects remain, but their torsions respond to a changing societal landscape, one in which queerness and contemporary art can no longer credibly claim to represent or inhabit a static "outside". Instead of romanticising or mourning Oiticica's resistant position, De Boeck re-sets it in motion – adapting its varying rhythms to the visual, sonic, economic and political landscapes of specific contemporary cultures.

From the solitary gyrations at documenta through the carnivalesque parade on the museum's grounds to the melancholy recitations at the art fair, De Boeck's *Parangolés* capture, as he puts it, "the intricate dance between action and reaction, stability and disruption."[21] They are transformative prisms through which spaces reveal their capacity to oppress and liberate, and the activated subjects the power to reinvent themselves and their worlds, however ephemerally. The twists and turns of De Boeck's queer interventions are inextricably individual and societal, physical and affective. Their power is circular, slowly drilling through institutional and psychological structures to get under their skin, to a space less defined, more emergent and open to the illogical spirals of becoming.

[21] Lieven De Boeck, email to the author, 19 August 2024.

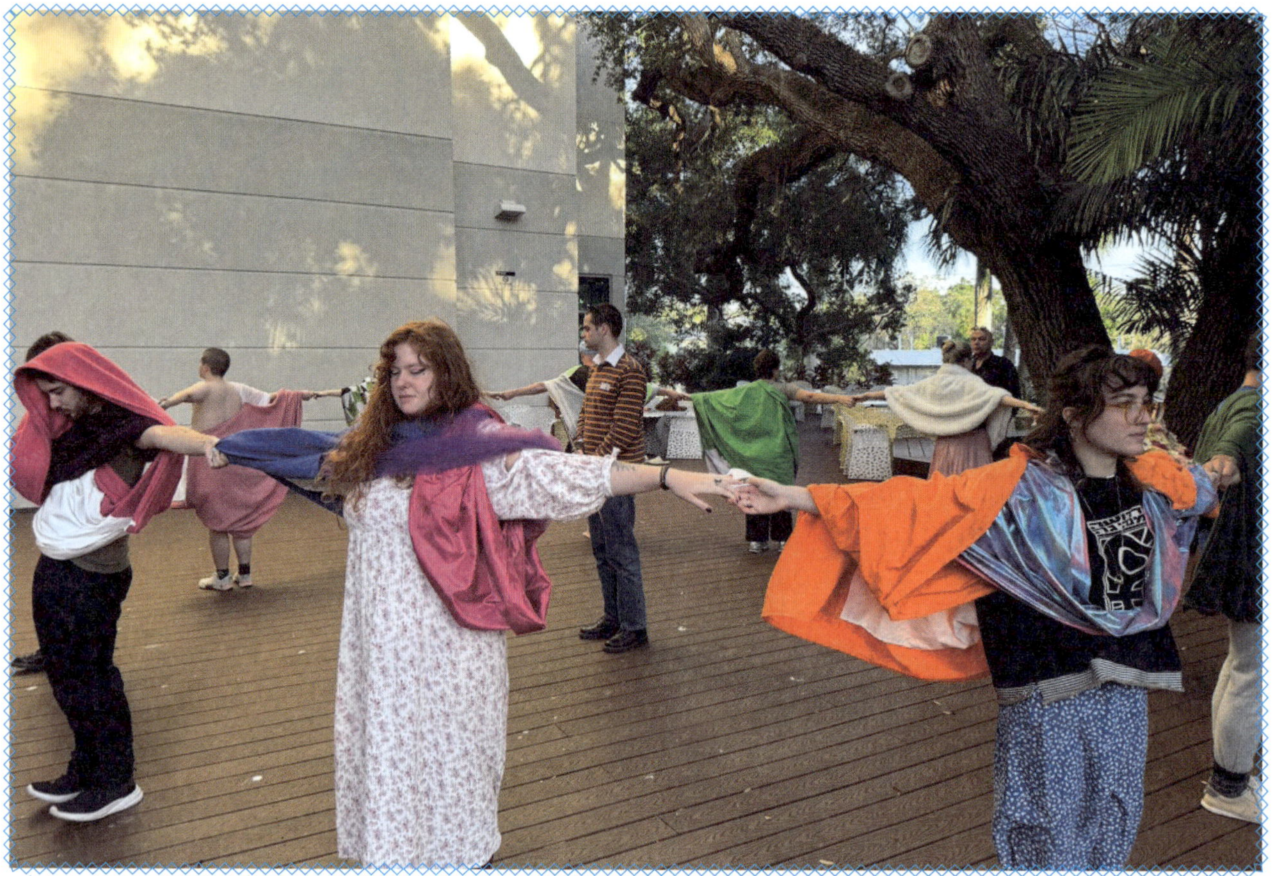

Campus Ringling College workshop try-out performance

Making of the costumes, Ringling Campus

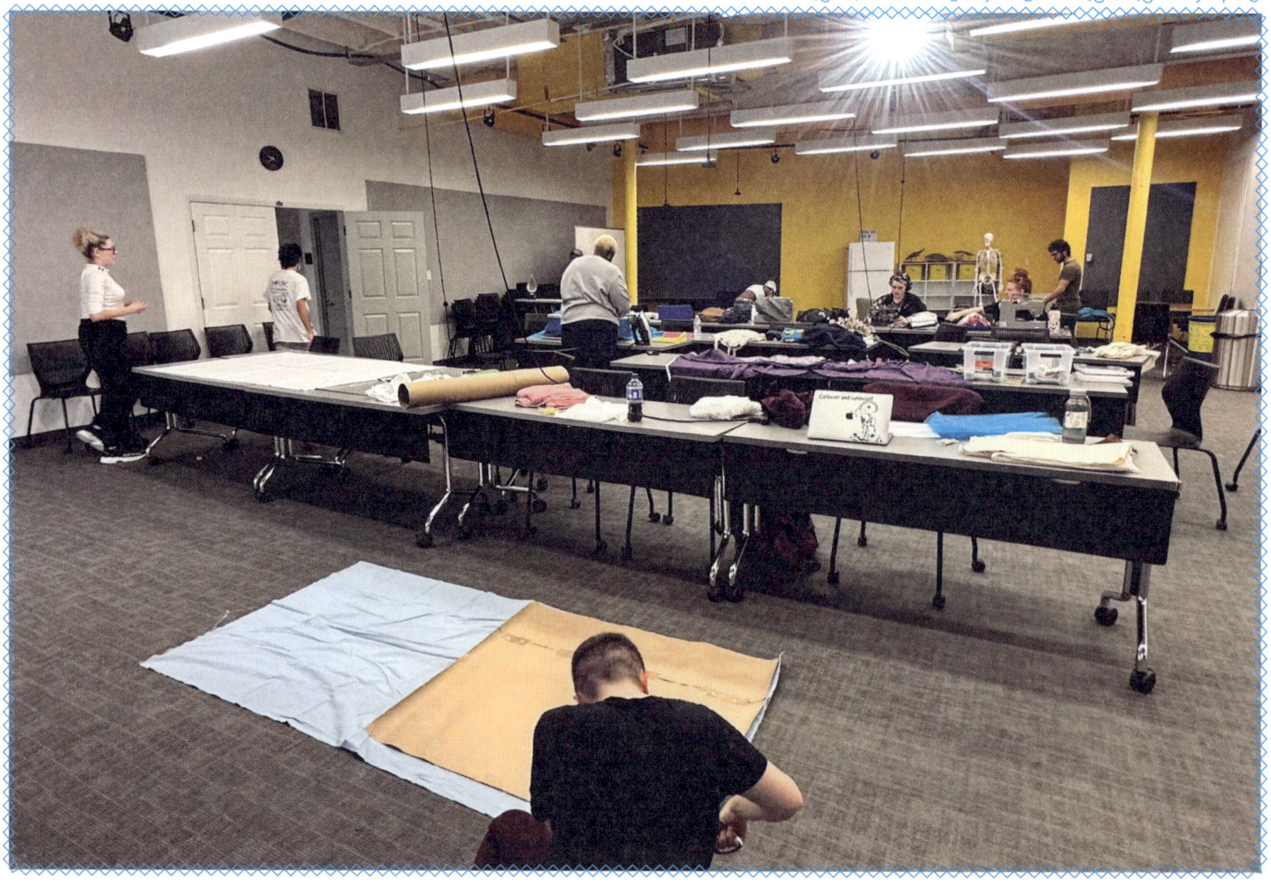

EXPERIMENT 01 - Ringling College of Art and Design

A collaborative project with Ringling College of Art and Design in Sarasota, Florida, was initiated to test the experiments developed in this manual for recreating and reactivating Parangolé Capa 21, Xoxoba by Hélio Oiticica. An open call invited students to participate in a two-part workshop, which involved crafting their own interpretations of the Parangolé cape, expressing each participant's gender identity, and activating the garments in a collective performance titled What's Going On?

Inspired by Oiticica's concepts of activation and co-authorship, the workshop allowed Ringling College students to create Parangolé-style costumes as a means of self-expression. Each student used a variety of materials, colors, and textures to design garments that embodied their gender or queer identities, transforming Oiticica's original work into a medium for personal exploration and celebration.

From August to November, the workshops—led by Lieven De Boeck, Marina Shaltout, and Sheryl Haler under the INDEX program—provided students with guidance on the creation of these distinctive costumes. Following the design phase, activation workshops in Sarasota offered participants the chance to engage further with Oiticica's legacy through movement and performance, adapting the performance specification form in the process. This experimentation helped refine the manual for both costume-making and the activation guidelines, enhancing their precision and flexibility.

The project concluded with public performances at the Sarasota Art Museum and the Untitled Art Fair during Art Basel Miami 2023. These events celebrated the intersection of identity, artistic expression, and community collaboration, culminating in the powerful collective performance What's Going On?

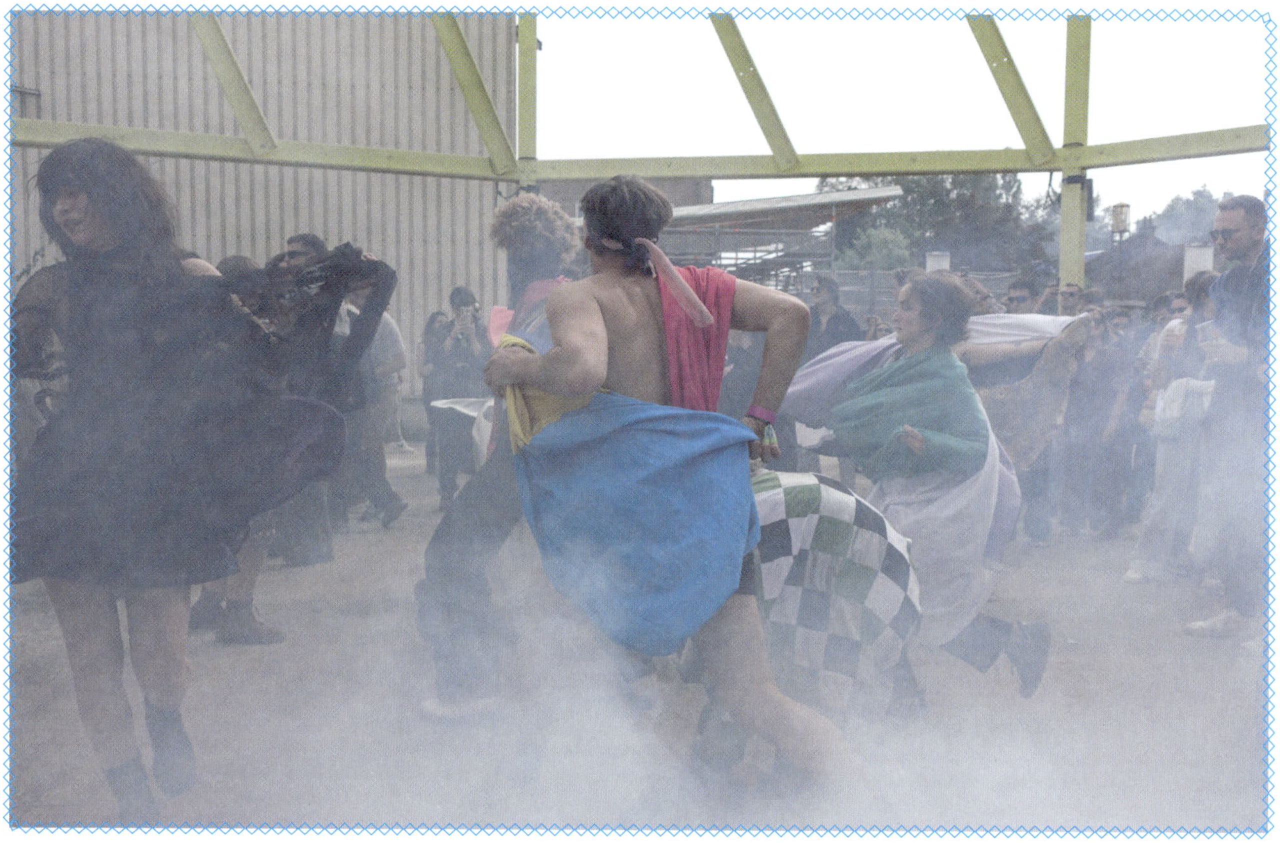

Main stage Horst festival

Group photo Horst festival

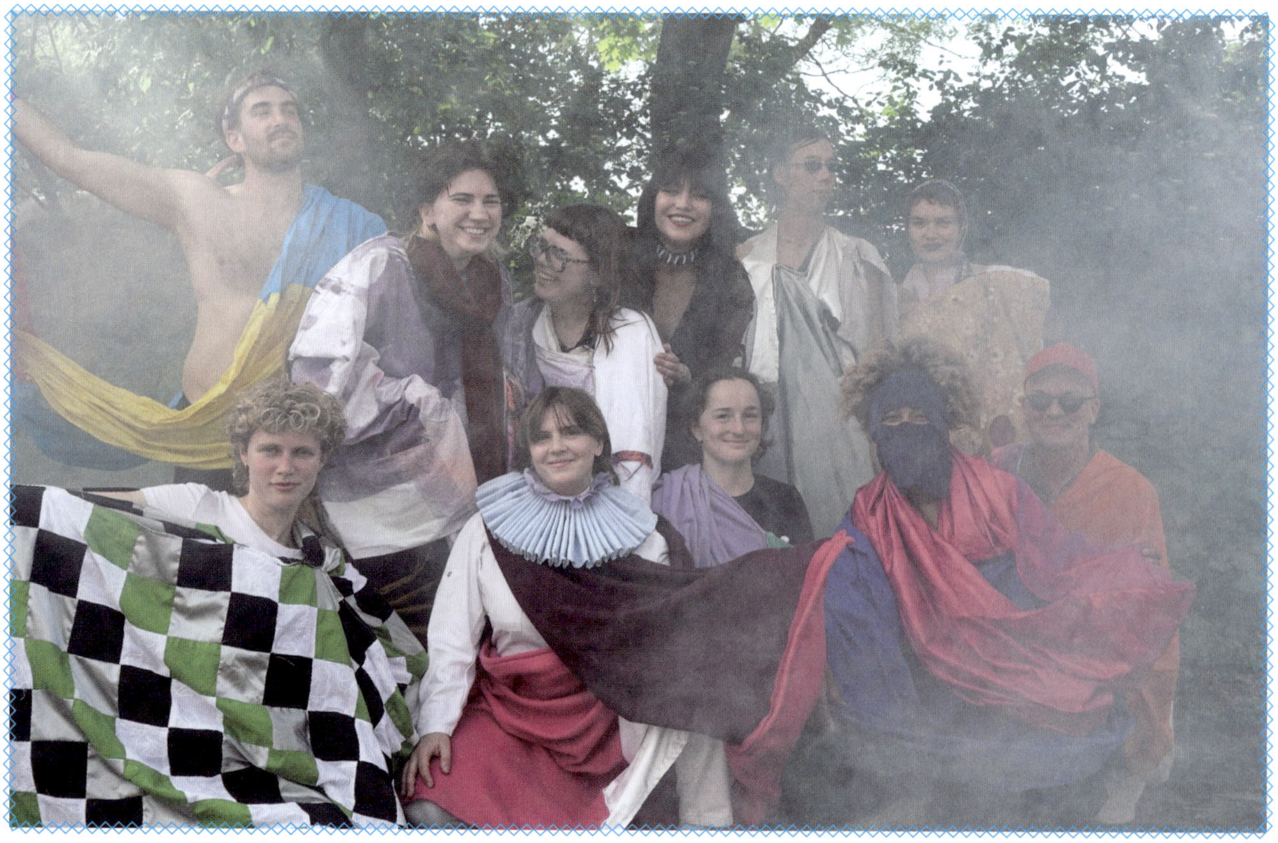

Experiment 02 - Horst Festival

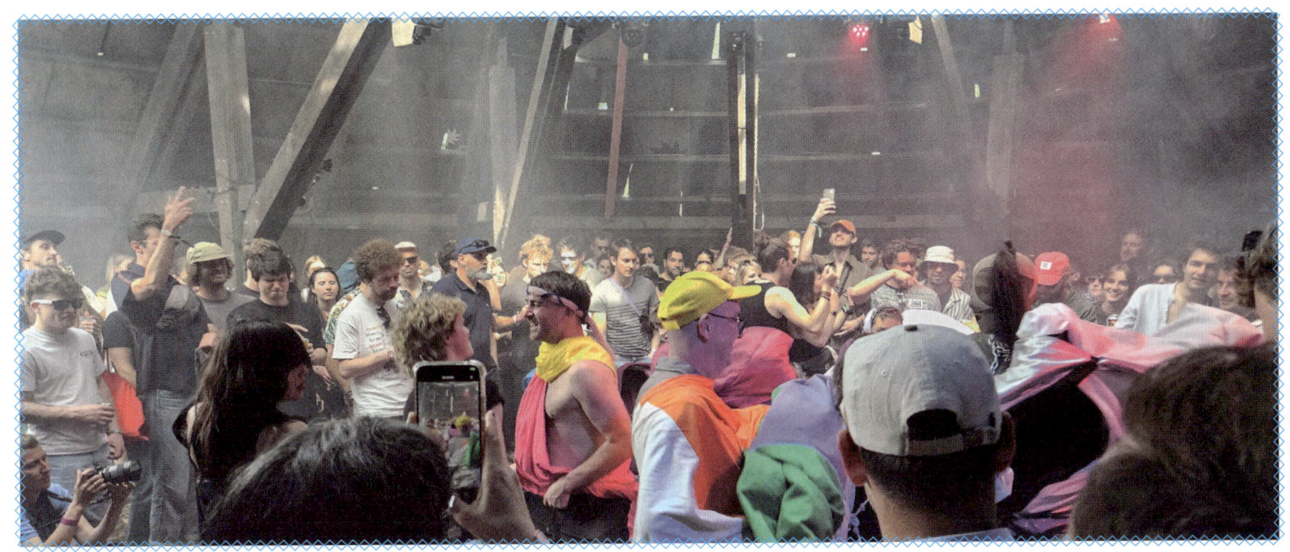

After the performances at the Sarasota Art Museum and Untitled Art Fair in Miami, where students from Ringling College of Art and Design first created the costumes, The Parade was reimagined at the HORST Arts & Music Festival. At HORST, participants actively engaged with the costumes, adding their own accessories to further personalize and transform the original designs.

The Parade at HORST evolved into a vibrant celebration of mixed-gender and queer identities. The performance became a dynamic and energetic spectacle that invited audience interaction, transforming it into a lively, immersive experience in a public space. This evolution resulted from a three-day workshop where festival attendees contributed their unique touches to the costumes, fostering a collaborative exchange of creativity and self-expression. The success of the public's participation was evident in the heartfelt letters from festival-goers to the Ringling students who had designed the costumes. Two of these letters are featured in this publication, reflecting the deep connections formed through this collaborative effort.

Through The Parade What's Going on?, I aimed to honor Brazilian artists Hélio Oiticica and Lygia Clark by transforming art into a participatory experience that thrives on personal engagement and community interaction. This process not only celebrated individuality but also redefined art as an evolving, interactive medium.

When is art? is the question Lieven De Boeck asks in his PhD thesis called *"The Archive of Disappearance, a Field Guide to Getting Lost,"* developed at the Hortence Research Centre of the Faculty of Architecture La Cambre–Horta of the Université libre de Bruxelles. His attempt to answer that question took the form of a performance that began when he, his studio assistant, a saxophone player, and a dozen Queer students from R^{ing}li_{ng} College of Art & Design in Sarasota, Florida, walked into the giant beach tent of the Untitled Art Fair in Miami Beach on December 6th, 2023. They performed The Parade, *What's going on?*–De Boeck's reactivation of a work by the late Hélio Oiticica, Brazilian artist and leader of the Neo–Concrete Movement (1960)–as if to demonstrate that the when of art is in the live remaking, not-reenacting, of it–in the impermanence of the present moment, but relevant to it.

From 1964–79, Oiticica created his *Parangolés* series consisting of colorful, multi-layered capes or 'costume paintings' made of layers of plastic and fabric, sometimes with objects and words, meant to be worn and danced in by everyday people to samba music, then the music of the underclass.
Oiticica was obsessed with samba and learned to dance in the Mangueira favela. He wanted to make visible the vibrant but marginalized, mostly Black culture that embraced him there through dance, which allowed one to be free of "excessive intellectualization." As a Queer man living in a heteronormative society made even less tolerant by the 1964 U.S.-backed military dictatorship in Brazil, being marginalized was a condition Oiticica felt and understood.

The Copy Is Original

Written by Bradley Wester

When dusted off and re-exhibited from the archive, historical artwork is meant to cement or occasionally alter the so-called historical narrative and distinguish it from the now. What disappears, however, is the nowness that once was.

The artwork as artifact is more like an exhumation. We may still appreciate it as art, but we must imagine its power and relevance for its time and context. In this way, it becomes more like an exact copy of itself.

When a historical art performance is performed again out of its time, it, too, is a copy of itself, a re-enactment, surrounded by historical context.

Just because it's performed live,

unfolding in real-time,

does not mean the work is still 'living.'

The archive, after all, is meant to catalog, preserve, and save the artwork

in perpetuity.

But might the distressing irony be

that the archive is where the artwork disappears and is lost?

Not always.

I recently had the opportunity to witness and participate in a living, resuscitated archive. This may seem like an oxymoron, but that is precisely what Belgian artist/ architect Lieven De Boeck proposes—how to remain faithful to a work of art from the past while making it relevant and alive in the present.

De Boeck likes to say of himself that he is *"a copy of the original."* Indeed, the words are tattooed on his left arm. His impulse to trouble the archive connects directly with his interest in reimagining his own art, often a staging of relational objects for continual renewal via various performative strategies. De Boeck: *"We mediate the work, but the reality of meaning lies in one's own interrelational presence between object and subject."* To not disappear into the archive, his work must be 'copy-able' for use in a continual state of nowness, of relational presence. Perhaps he really means 'the copy becomes the original,' that each new iteration of the work becomes the original again and again.

An un-archivable work that resists classification and calcification! I identify this formal device of continuous renewal as utopic and Queer. Unable to fit in, the work is encountered, expelled, and renewed.

When remembering his childhood, De Boeck speaks of an early sense of not belonging, an almost universal story for the Queer-identified across generations. Even before cognition is the sense of not belonging, the threat of violent repercussions, and the profound pressure to disappear.

For some, suicide is an extreme choice. The Queer Closet, historically, is a more common response that creates a copy of oneself for external consumption and self-preservation. Here, life is performance to preserve life, less a copy and more a counterfeit—for many, the original is lost forever, archived. For others, especially for creatives like De Boeck, these early Queer experiences reinforce Queer desire. They are transformed into powerful tools for potential world-making—making an improved copy of the original. No, De Boeck's work is not about Queer Identity politics; it's much too generous and democratic than that.

What is a copy if not for everyone?

De Boeck is interested in making a thing that can never be archived because potential is something yet to be created. There can be completions, but only to be replayed/renewed by the following participant/observer.

Such a work radically resists the *'archive of disappearance.'* This is the Queer architect in him, too—a building is immaterial unless as a living, breathing expression of its use and interaction with its inhabitants and what they create inside it.

How can we perform the *Parangolés* today

and

make it relevant to the present vis-à-vis contemporary Queerness within another native tropical environment like Brazil's?

De Boeck's solution was to apply Oiticica's experience to his own Queer identity and the politics of the now, including his recruitment of a dozen Queer-identified Ringling students across disciplines to create their own *Parangolés* based on personal interpretations of Queer flags in their tropical state of Florida.

The Ringling students' joy was palpable as they began to move improvisationally, their bulky, somewhat awkward-looking *Parangolés* (which the students made themselves) unfolding and billowing into lavish sensuousness within the neoliberal contemporary art fair space, where merchandise, primarily in the form of paintings, hung lifeless in comparison. Joy engulfed the onlookers, too, and some became performers when several students removed their capes and proffered them.

Most striking to me, also a Queer artist and writer, was the full-circle, cross-generational aspect of this living reenactment. Four generations of Queer sensibility were contained in this project: Oiticica's 1960s, my 1970s–80s (both of us experiencing our Queerness when the acts were still illegal), De Boeck's 90s–00s, and the undergraduate Ringling students today, many of whom only recently out. Completing the conceptual circle is Florida's current state of conservative politics, closer to Oiticica's Brazil every day.

A recent Pen America study shows that 40% of all banned books in America's school libraries occurred in Florida, with thousands of those books by or about Black or LGBTQ authors or characters. Two of Florida's most famous presidential candidates speak in the language of dictatorships.

...And yet, I don't see the work of Lieven De Boeck as being about 'Identity Politics.' It is far more expansive and philosophical than that self-reflexive reduction. A shared Queerness was simply a way to revitalize Oiticica's work.

But I am interested in how the logics and methods of his larger body of work are Queer.

Indeed, in one work De Boeck creates components for participants to arrange building blocks. We become builders of Lego-imagined architectures that can be assembled and dissembled—the pleasure of this experience is contingent on favoring the question over the answer. Nothing is fixed; all things are transmutable. There are only questions ripe with potential.

I am writing this from Venice while also covering the pre-opening of the 60th Venice Biennale Arte Exhibition titled "Foreigners Everywhere," curated by Adriano Pedrosa. He includes many groups in the diaspora of foreigners—refugees, indigenous, the 'global south,' so-called "naive," "outsider," and the "self-taught." Pedrosa also includes Queer populations. I believe Pedrosa intends to show us the agency of Queer desire, its utopic impulse. Ostensibly, to show us the agency of all so-called 'foreigners.'
Alas, I'm certain artists of the Global South, Indigenous and Queer artists don't see themselves as foreign. So what happens to that agency of 'the foreign' when the exhibition is meant for the Global North's gaze, when its design and format are so familiar, established, and institutionalized as the Venice Biennale...? Making the foreign familiar (to the Global North) defeats the purpose.

This is the same format mistake made by the LGBTQ+ movement
(powered by mostly affluent gay white males)
to make heteronormative marriage rights a priority.
It's the same mistake made by many well-intentioned, post-BLM monuments
of inclusion that attempt to mark the victims, unsung heroes of the global slave
trade—bronze plaques and statues in the same format as the oppressor. Like the
statues recently torn down, only with thicker-lipped faces and by artists of color.
What does an un-monument look like?
A truly Queer union?
And how does a Queer or Foreign exhibition be queer and foreign while giving
everyone access..?

We may find a clue within the strategies of artist Lieven De Boeck.

Dear Sammy,

As a child, I was already betrayed by my voice and my gestures. They said I was different. My mother said I was more sensitive. Manners, no friends. At the moment I decided not to lie to them anymore and to tear doubt from their venomous mouths, it was too late to turn back. I saw fear in the eyes of the barbaric children, but I also felt comforting hands. I no longer wanted to hug the walls and count the tiles on the floor, my head tucked into my frail shoulders. It was no longer about surviving, but about living, about invading space. I dressed myself in armor that I polished and adorned with glitter, pink, and pearl. I sewed it to my skin and gave it my name. When I went outside, I could be both a queen and their monster, but I existed.

When we collectively discovered the Parangolés, carefully wrapped in plastic pouches, my gaze immediately fell on the velvety satin material that reflected the absent light of the hangar. I felt like I was holding in my hands the armor I wore as a teenager. It was as if it belonged to my body.

Silver-gray like the cold and bright light of Christmas mornings, the textile reminded me of my mother's gentle hands that catch you after a fall. Already in my hands, I felt its protective potential.

When I put on the costume, I felt a brutal, almost violent, reversal; I felt ridiculous. I felt ashamed in the eyes of others. I, who thought I was putting on armor, felt like I was wearing chains. Heavy, uncomfortable, they limited my movements, made me mute, timid. Dancing in front of a crowd where everything is vast, I became that feverish child again. My body curled up, tight; it only expressed itself through the discomfort of being too much. I saw others move with ease, enter into harmony, into dialogue. I, I only heard

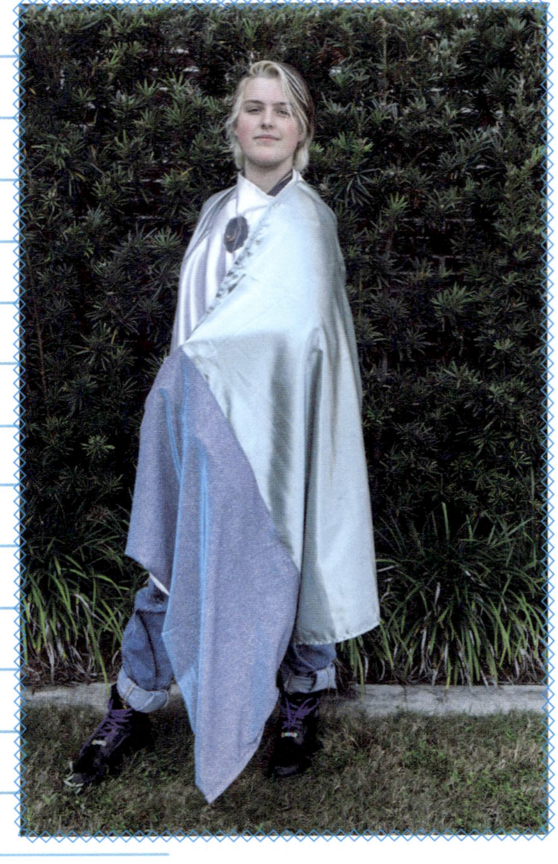

silence and incomprehension. It took me time to understand the costume, its weight, its potential for movement, its malleability. Nothing was obvious anymore,as if I was starting from scratch. But it seems that I found satisfaction in reacquainting myself with what seemed acquired, in reconsidering other seduction alternatives, in considering my body not only through my own interests, but also taking into account those of others, their energies, their feelings. To change the terms of this armor, to be more empathetic, more attentive, and less mischievous.

For the performance, I wanted my accessory to reflect that initial sensation when I put on the costume, so I covered my face with stockings and wrapped steel chains around my neck. Inflicting this feeling of suffocation, but which revealed a great freedom. I was unidentifiable. But it allowed me to be more comfortable, freer in my movements, to be non-binary, monstrous, sexual, strange, and at the same time to feel powerful, limitless, and free. I found it exhilarating to give an identity to anonymity and to make it dialogue with the public and the other performers. There was something transcendental when I no longer made a distinction between the character and my body embodying the character. We were carried by each other, and our bodies collided, attracted, then repelled each other in a movement both personal and collective, forming an atomic microcosm.

Our bodies belonged to us and at the same time, we gave ourselves for others. Without judgment, without apprehensions, we could be both monsters and queens.

Thank you, the glitter still sticks to my skin.

Toàn,

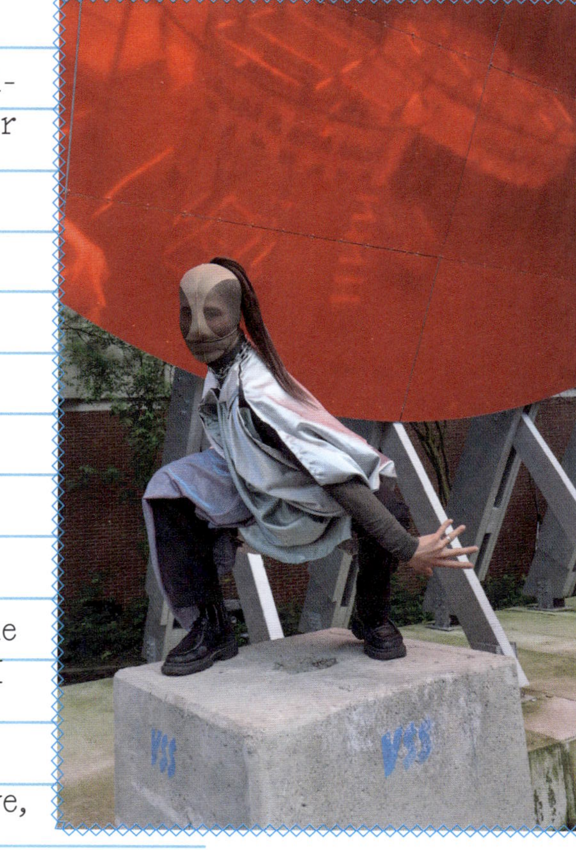

Dear Viv,

First of all, I apologize for not writing sooner. You've been on my mind since I wore your outfit, but life got in the way, and it felt as though I'd drifted far from the happy bubble of that performance.

There's something poetic about planting seeds and the time it takes for them to bloom—it feels like a metaphor for both your outfit and my delay in writing to you.

I've been trying to find the right way to share the impression your outfit left on me during those performances at the Horst Festival.

The intricacy of the patterns and fabric combinations you chose stood out to me. It carries an uplifting, poetic spirit, yet its heaviness, its oversized and lavish but slightly impractical design, held such depth. I think that's what drew me to your costume—the contrasts it embodied. It spoke of joy and lightness but also of weight and grounding. It felt like a reminder: flowers don't bloom out of nowhere; joy and brightness are rooted in struggle. It made me think of Tupac's words: "The rose that grew from concrete."

Maybe I'm overthinking it, but wearing your costume felt like a way of meeting you, of reading what was important to you at the time of its creation. In any case, I'm deeply grateful for this ghostly connection—a chance to channel a relationship with someone I don't know by inhabiting their colors, their flowers, their weight. I felt regal and strange (a strangeness that felt like home), all at once. My movements shifted between grounded stances and swirling the fabric around me, letting it float.

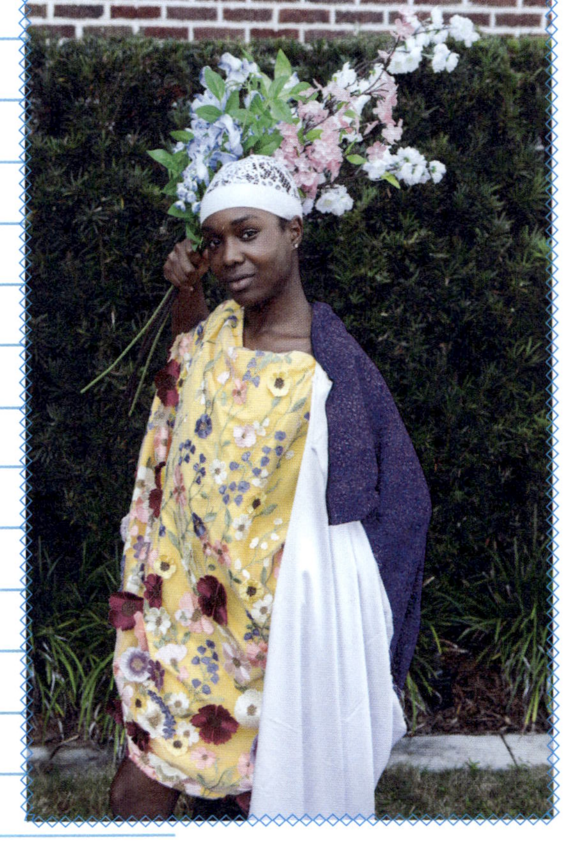

There was also something cocoon-like about the costume—a chrysalis,
offering a layer of protection during a moment of transition.
That feeling was so soothing.

The parade itself felt like a soft gathering, a promise of togetherness that
created space to daydream, to step away from the logic of compliance or
compromise. I loved its openness—it felt as though we became an offering to
the people at the festival, a reminder to tap into joy as a source of life. There
were so many smiles, and a couple of memorable dances that still linger with
me.

It felt like holding onto circular time, marking the present with an invitation
to be, to feel, to surrender.

I've also been thinking about how "Vi" with an e echoes the French word for
life—vie. That connection felt alive in your costume too, as though it held a re-
flection of freedom and the layered possibilities of being alive, of joy as a fer-
tile, rooted experience. It also brought me closer to my love for carnival—the
nostalgia, expansiveness, and transgressive joy it offers. (I've always had
a deep attachment to it, maybe because I'm half Brazilian.)

I hope that in some way, my dancing stayed within your costume, that it
carries traces of how happy I felt while wearing it.

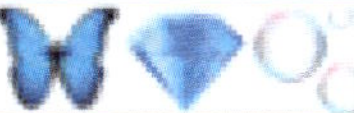

Thank you,

Juliette

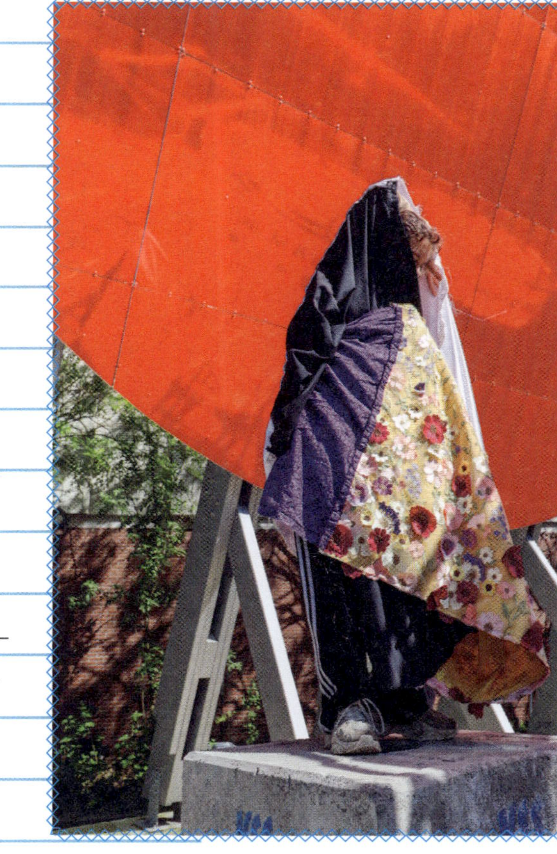

Ultimately, this manual stands as a celebration of the power of collective creativity. It underscores the importance of creating spaces where art, identity, and community intersect, allowing for authentic and dynamic expressions. The journey detailed within these pages reaffirms that art, when approached through a collaborative and queer lens, can continuously evolve, reflect, and resonate in ever-changing contexts.

A Responsability

by ldb⁺

This manual embodies the profound synergy achieved through the collaborative efforts of diverse participants and varied contexts.

The exploration of queer temporality and artistic practice described within these pages is a testament to a collective journey spanning academic, artistic, and experiential realms.

The insights presented here are not solely the product of a singular perspective but are enriched by the contributions and interactions of numerous individuals and settings. From the initial conceptualization of *"The Archive of Disappearance"* to its current iteration, the manual reflects, as explained in the introduction, a dynamic interplay between personal experiences and collaborative research.
Engaging with Hélio Oiticica's works, activating them through reinterpretations, and incorporating feedback from participants have all played crucial roles in shaping this exploration.

The experiences shared by students, artists, and festival participants illustrate how art can transcend traditional boundaries when approached with an openness to diverse perspectives. The process of creating new *Parangolés*, activating them in various contexts, and inviting public engagement has demonstrated the transformative potential of collaborative artistic practices.

The manual highlights how queer temporality and post-productive approaches challenge conventional norms, offering fresh ways to understand and experience art.

Colophon

Set Margins' #36

Breaking Free:
Queer Temporality and Collaborative Art

By LDB[+]

ISBN: 978-90-834498-3-8

Editor: LDB[+]
Contributing authors: LDB[+], Bradley Wester, Antony Hudek
Graphic design: Freek Lomme i.c.w. LDB[+]
Printer: Booxs, Den Bosch (NL)
Project management: Kurt Vanbelleghem and Freek Lomme
Photography: Photos Final Costumes: Antoine Doetsch
                                   Photos Manual Making costumes: Studio Ester
                                   Goris
                                   Photos Parade Sarasota: Harry Sayer
                                   Photos Parade Horst: Biuk
                                   Cover photo: Hadrien Duré
                                   Other photos: studio LDB[+]
Lithography (selected):   SebastiaanHanekroot / Colour and Books
Fonts: Edition Contextual and Edition Asymetrical by
                                   Elias Hanzer, Ductus by Amélie Dumont /
                                   Bye Bye Binary, Antipasto by Zetafonts.

Made possible thanks to

Thank you

I would like to express my deepest gratitude to everyone who made this project and publication possible. These are the culmination of ideas initially explored in my PhD research, *The Archive of Disappearance, a Field Guide to Getting Lost*, conducted at the Hortence Research Lab, Faculty of Architecture, ULB, Brussels, under the inspiring guidance of Wouter Van Acker.

This publication reflects on *The Parade: What's Going On?*, a work developed with the invaluable support and direction of Kurt Vanbelleghem.

I am especially thankful to Ringling College of Art and Design for their boundless enthusiasm and unwavering support, particularly to Jeff Schwartz, Associate Vice President and Dean of Undergraduate Studies, whose encourage- ment was truly indispensable. I also extend my heartfelt thanks to Marina Shaltout and Sheryl Haler for their vital roles in the costume workshops. My gratitude extends to Elcin Haskollar, Dean of Inclusion, as well as the Sarasota Art Museum and Chief Curator Rangsook Yoon for graciously hosting the final rehearsal of *The Parade: What's Going On?*.

I am equally grateful to the participating students of Ringling College, whose openness and creative courage brought the parade to life. Special thanks to Clara Andrade Pereira and Omar López-Chahoud from the Untitled Art Fair for inviting us to perform at their 2023 Miami event, which was an unforgettable opportunity.

A big thank you to Bradley Wester, who participated in the Sarasota workshops, later joined us in Miami for the performance, and contributed a wonderful text to this publication.

I am also deeply appreciative of Louise Goegebeur for the invitation to the Horst Festival, where I had the privilege of conducting both a workshop and a performance over the three-day festival, further enriching the parade's evolution. Thanks to the participants, Antoine, Toan, Maj-Britt, Annelise, Zarina, Emma, Marie, Juliette.

To my assistant, Emma Revest, thank you for your unwavering dedication throughout this journey. I am also incredibly grateful to Studio Ester Goris for helping to finalise the final costumes. My appreciation goes to Zarina, Noé, Oscar, Anne-Sophie, Bryn, Guillaume, and Maxime for bringing the costumes to life at the seaside, and to Antoine Doetsch for brilliantly capturing these moments in photographs.

Finally, I would like to express my profound gratitude to Antony Hudek for his steadfast belief in my artistic practice and his thoughtful contribution in the text 'Twist and Turns' as well as to Freek Lomme for his constant encouragement and for agreeing to publish this book.